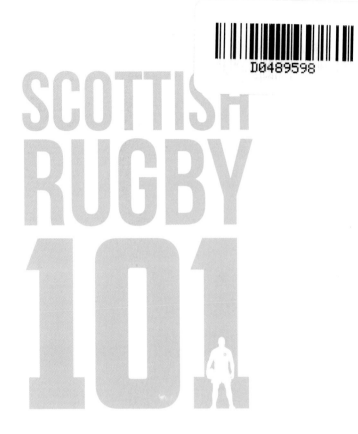

SCOTTISH
RUGBY
101

SCOTTISH RUGBY 101

A POCKET GUIDE
IN 101 MOMENTS, STATS, CHARACTERS AND GAMES

PETER BURNS

This edition first published in 2018 by

POLARIS PUBLISHING LTD
c/o Turcan Connell
Princes Exchange
1 Earl Grey Street
Edinburgh
EH3 9EE

in association with

ARENA SPORT
An imprint of Birlinn Limited
West Newington House
10 Newington Road
Edinburgh
EH9 1QS

www.polarispublishing.com
www.arenasportbooks.co.uk

ISBN: 9781909715677
eBook ISBN: 9781788851091

British Library Cataloguing-in-Publication Data
A catalogue record for this book is available on request from the British Library.

Designed and typeset by Polaris Publishing, Edinburgh

Printed in Great Britain by MBM Print SCS Limited, East Kilbride

For Julie, Isla and Hector.

Thank you for putting up with so much rugby.

ACKNOWLEDGEMENTS

I AM indebted to a number of sources, but most notably to the doyen of British rugby history, John Griffiths, for his advice, entry suggestions and proof-reading, and to Isobel Irvine for supplying such a wonderful entry on the history of Scotland women's Test rugby. The ESPN Scrum website, which is a treasure-trove of stats and records, as well as Keith Young's *The Complete Rugby Union Compendium*, Kenneth Bogle's *Scottish Rugby: Game by Game*, *A Portrait of Scottish Rugby* by Allan Massie and *The Thistle: A Chronicle of Scottish Rugby* by Derek Douglas have all been a huge help. Finally, thank you to David Barnes, who wrote *Behind the Thistle: Playing Rugby for Scotland* with me, which has been a great reference when putting this book together. It's quite a nice feeling to be able to refer to your own book when writing a new one.

INTRODUCTION

I REMEMBER the first time I went to Murrayfield. It was 17 February 1990, to watch Scotland defeat France 21–0. I was there again on 17 March, overwhelmed by the noise and emotion of the Championship's final game as Scotland edged a titanic battle with England to take only the third Grand Slam in our history.

It was a terrible time to fall in love with Scottish rugby – when we were really, really good. I would go to watch Scotland and, more often than not, we would win. Being young and naive, I thought that that was how it had always been – and, worse, how it would always be. It was only later that I discovered that my confidence had virtually zero correlation with the fortunes enjoyed by the team during the previous 120 years. But as a nine-year-old in the spring of 1990, I was ignorant of Scottish rugby's difficult past and unrealistically optimistic about the future. Halcyon days indeed; like the happy years of believing in Santa Claus – idyllic, magical . . . short.

Although the seasons that immediately followed 1990 were by and large positive, there were some sobering defeats to the top five teams in the world (New Zealand, South Africa, Australia, England and France) and come the millennium, the hard years had returned again.

Since lifting the last ever Five Nations trophy in 1999, being a Scottish rugby fan has often been a pretty grim experience. There have been the odd rays of sunshine, of course – the results ledger shows that every major nation in the world, bar New Zealand, has been defeated since the turn of the century – and how agonisingly close Scotland came to breaking their duck against the All Blacks in November 2017. And after the foundations laid by Vern Cotter and with the form being shown under the stewardship of Gregor Townsend, it feels like we are back among the contenders again. Long may it continue. But a stark reality remains – ever since its inception, we've struggled to put together a meaningful challenge for the Six Nations. And Grand Slams and World Cups? Forget it. Not even close.

But here's the thing. That love, that first burst into life as I sat in the east stand with my dad, watching the train race by behind the south terrace before kick-off and then becoming one with a crowd that shifted, swelled and roared for a glorious hour and a half as we watched Scotland take their first step towards that wondrous 1990 Grand Slam . . . that love has never waned. Not once. Not even after some of the worst defeats.

My dad and I came home after that France match and watched the recording of the BBC's coverage, Bill McLaren's rolling cadences and the TV angles adding another dimension to my memories. In the days that followed, I began what became a lifelong habit of devouring every piece of rugby writing I could lay my hands on. Match reports, analyses, histories and biographies. I would watch *101 Greatest Tries* and *Another 101 Greatest Tries* on VHS over and over and over again. I wanted to know everything about the game and the players, to understand what had happened in previous encounters and so begin to dream about the matches to come.

When the 1990 Grand Slam video came out at the end of the season, I watched it on loop. Then I went back and watched the 1984 Grand Slam video, discovering another generation of heroes.

Rugby autobiographies, biographies and histories have shuffled unceasingly across my bedside table ever since. It sometimes feels like I've read every rugby book that's been published since the 1980s – and I've delved back well before then as well. I even read Rupert Moon's *Full Moon*. I bet not many people in Scotland can claim to have done that. How about Will Carling's *England Dream Team*? Or *The Good the Bad and the Rugby* by Tony Ward? Peter FitzSimons' *Basking in Beirut and Other Adventures*? Anyone else out there read those? They're actually pretty good (well, maybe not Carling's).

And the end result of all of this? I am in possession of an astonishing amount of dull rugby trivia. Not a great selling-point for this book, I admit . . . but here's the rub. I have gathered all I know about Scottish rugby and I have distilled it, curating this little handbook from my mental museum – a 101 crib-sheet to Scottish rugby for the more rational and sensible of you out there who are Scotland supporters, who love the game and the jersey and the players, but who are hopefully less all-consumed by it. Meanwhile, I look forward to hearing (do I?) from the other rugby bores who want to debate my choices or argue a point or two. I'm pretty confident there will be a few contentious issues in here. So here we go: 101 moments, stats, facts, characters and games gathered from 150-odd years of Scottish Test rugby.

Crouch. Bind . . . Enjoy.

'Hey you guys, I have a game we could play . . .'

Scotland's grand rugby adventure began way back in 1854 when two brothers, Alexander and Francis Crombie, moved from Durham to Edinburgh and brought the rules of a fascinating new game with them. Francis enrolled at the Edinburgh Academy and began spreading the rugby gospel. Thanks to his influence, within three years the game had reached Merchiston Castle School and the Royal High School of Edinburgh.

The first inter-school game in Scotland was played between Merchiston and the High School of Edinburgh on 13 February 1858. Merchiston then played Edinburgh Academy at Raeburn Place in December that same year – a match that has been played every year since, making it the oldest continuous fixture in the world.

FAMOUS FIRSTS

Scotland's oldest club

While Francis Crombie was pioneering rugby at the Edinburgh Academy, his brother Alexander helped set up the Edinburgh Academicals Football Club in 1857 for former pupils of the school and became the club's first captain, from 1858 to 1864. Edinburgh Accies are the second oldest club in the world (the Trinity Club, now known as Dublin University, claim to be the oldest club, having first played in 1854) and have produced more than 127 Scotland Test players – second only to London Scottish.

1857

FAMOUS FIRSTS

The first Test match

The first ever rugby union international was played between Scotland and England at Raeburn Place in Edinburgh (Edinburgh Accies' home ground) on 27 March 1871. It was 20-a-side and Scotland's line-up consisted of 14 forwards, three half-backs and three full-backs; England, meanwhile, selected 13 forwards, three half-backs, one three-quarter-back and three full-backs. Scotland won the match by one goal and one try to one try. In those days, taking the ball across the opposition's line earned the attacking team a try at goal (hence the word 'try').

Scotland's first Test team.

4

Oh captain, my captain

Francis Moncreiff was handed the honour of being Scotland's first Test rugby captain. Moncreiff – the son of James Moncreiff, 1st Baron Moncreiff of Tullibole – was a former pupil of the Edinburgh Academy, a chartered accountant by profession, and had played a central role in the staging of the first Test. In March 1870, a football match between Scotland and England was played at The Oval in Surrey, with a rematch played in November that same year. However, there was some disquiet north of the border because these games had been played under English FA rules which, at the time, were practised by only four clubs in Scotland. In December 1870, a letter was published in *Bell's Life in London* and signed by the captains of five senior clubs (including Moncreiff, who was captain of Edinburgh Accies), challenging 'any team selected from the whole of England to play us a match, twenty-a-side, rugby rules either in Edinburgh or Glasgow on any day during the present season that might be suitable to the English players'. And so it all began.

Moncreiff would win a total of three caps against England, finishing his career with one win, one loss and a draw to his name. He died in Edinburgh in 1900, aged 50.

FAMOUS FIRSTS

Pioneering diversity

When Joe Ansbro made his Test debut in 2010 many of the headlines surrounding his selection focused on the fact that he was the first black player to represent Scotland at rugby union. Ansbro was not, however, the first player of colour to play for Scotland; in the very first Test match, Alfred Clunies-Ross, who was of mixed Scottish and Indonesian origin, won his solitary cap as one of the three full-backs. Ross was born in the Cocos Islands (also known as the Keeling Islands – a small archipelago in the Indian Ocean midway between Australia and Sri Lanka) in 1851. He was the son of John Clunies-Ross from the Shetland Islands and S'pia Dupong from Surakarta in Central Java. Alfred and his brothers were schooled at Madras College in St Andrews before Alfred went on to study medicine at Edinburgh University. He moved to London in 1873 to work at St George's Hospital and, although he never again wore the blue of Scotland, he played with distinction for Wasps from 1874 until his retirement from the game in 1880.

The creation of the SRU

The Scottish Football Union (later to be rebranded as the Scottish Rugby Union in 1924) came into existence in 1873. The founder members were:

Edinburgh Academicals	Edinburgh University
Glasgow Academicals	Glasgow University
Merchistonians	The Royal High School FP
St Andrews University	West of Scotland

Curiously, five of the founding clubs were already members of the RFU. Because there was no national union in existence in Scotland, Edinburgh University, Glasgow Academicals and West of Scotland had joined the RFU in 1871, and Edinburgh Academicals and Royal High School FP had joined in 1872 – but they renounced their membership when the SFU was founded.

While the RFU is the oldest existing union, the SFU were pioneers in founding the International Rugby Football Board, now known as World Rugby, in 1886 with Ireland and Wales, with England joining in 1890.

7

Babes in arms

Dates of birth are not available for all of those who have played Test rugby for Scotland, but among the Five Nations and Tri-Nations, the youngest player to be capped to date is Ninian Finlay, who was 17 years and 36 days when he played against England in 1875. His compatriot Charles Reid was also 17 years and 36 days on his debut against Ireland in 1888, however Reid was technically a day older than Finlay on debut, having lived through an extra leap-day.

The ten youngest players to appear for Scotland are:

Name	Age on debut	Opposition	Date
1. NJ Finlay	17y 36d	England	8 Mar 1875
2. C Reid	17y 36d	Ireland	19 Feb 1881
3. WG Neilson	17y 167d	England	17 Mar 1894
4. W Neilson	17y 173d	Wales	7 Feb 1891
5. KG MacLeod	17y 289d	New Zealand	18 Nov 1905
6. LM Balfour-Melville	17y 333d	England	5 Feb 1872
7. A Arthur	17y 339d	England	8 Mar 1875
8. RW Irvine	17y 342d	England	27 Mar 1871
9. DM Grant	18y 36d	Wales	4 Feb 1911
10. MW Walter	18y 51d	Ireland	24 Feb 1906

8

The first full-back

The first player to take up the lone position of full-back in a Test match was Henry Johnston against Ireland in 1877. Scotland won the match in Belfast with Robert Mackenzie scoring a hat-trick of tries to accompany efforts from Bulldog Irvine, Edward Pocock and James Reid, with Malcolm Cross converting four of these and Mackenzie slotting two drop-goals. Johnston retained his place at full-back when Scotland faced England at Raeburn Place two weeks later. Cross was once again the hero of the day, dropping a goal for the only points of the match, but the victory would prove to be Johnston's last cap. He qualified as a doctor from Edinburgh University in 1880 and had a long and distinguished career as an army surgeon and a renowned botanist before his death in Orkney in 1939.

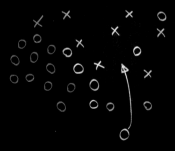

The Border Bull

Adam Dalgleish was the first player from the Borders to be capped for Scotland, making his debut against Wales in Cardiff in February 1890. A local hero at his club Gala, where he played from 1886 to 1896 (and captained them for three seasons), he went on to win eight caps over four seasons of Test rugby, winning four and losing four. Nominally a forward, he was an excellent sevens player and was skilful enough to often play in the backs. His obituary in the *Scotsman* heralded him as 'a great forward, and although he never weighed heavier than 11 stones 9 lbs, was strong and sturdy'. He was made Gala's first life member in July 1935, three years before his death at his home in the Border town in September 1938, aged 70.

10

The Triple Crown

Scotland won its first Triple Crown in 1891. Wales travelled to Edinburgh in February for the first match of the Home Union Championship and were met by a ferocious Scottish side who scored seven tries, one conversion and two drop-goals to secure a 15–0 victory. Two weeks later, Scotland travelled to Belfast to face Ireland and were again rampant, scoring five tries, three conversions and a drop-goal in a 14–0 win. The Triple Crown was wrapped up at Richmond on 7 March when tries by Willie Neilson and Jack Orr were converted by the excellently named Gregor MacGregor and Paul Clauss dropped a goal in a 9–3 win.

11

FAMOUS FIRSTS

The Border League

In 1901, Gala, Hawick, Langholm, Melrose and Jed-forest banded together to form the world's first competitive rugby union league. The proposal for the league was initially viewed with suspicion by the Scottish Football Union (the predecessor to the SRU), who feared that the organisation of meaningful fixtures over friendlies went against the Corinthian spirit of the game, but they eventually relented and sanctioned the league's formation.

The league expanded in 1912 to include Selkirk and Kelso and was enlarged again in 1996 with the inclusion of Peebles; Berwick and Duns and Hawick YM have all had stints in the league in the years since, although each has subsequently dropped out (along with Langholm) to leave the current make-up of Gala, Hawick, Jed-forest, Kelso, Melrose, Peebles and Selkirk contesting for the title.

12

A game of numbers

Rugby was a 20-a-side game until a petition was begun by the SFU to reduce the numbers to 15. This was eventually accepted by the other Home Unions and the change in playing numbers came into effect in 1877.

The Scottish Rugby Menagerie

Two of the early stars of Scottish rugby also had two of the best nicknames in the sport – Charles 'Hippo' Reid and Robert 'Bulldog' Irvine. Hippo Reid is the joint youngest player to play for Scotland (see fact number 7) and was still at school when he made his debut against Ireland in 1881. He won 21 caps in a seven-year international career, while Bulldog Irvine won 13 caps between 1871 and 1880 and captained the team on eight occasions. Over the years, they have been joined in the Scottish Rugby Menagerie by Ian 'Mighty Mouse' McLauchlan and Iain 'the Bear' Milne. The Mouse won 51 caps in a fearsome career that saw him etch his name in rugby legend with his contribution to the Lions' tour victories over New Zealand in 1971 and South Africa in 1974. The Bear was also a Lion, touring New Zealand in 1983, and winning 44 caps over a Test career that spanned the years 1979 to 1990, which included a seismic contribution to Scotland's Grand Slam triumph in 1984.

14

FAMOUS FIRSTS

The butcher's boy's bright idea

In 1883, Melrose Football Club were looking for ways to raise funds when Ned Haig, an apprentice local butcher, suggested the idea of a seven-a-side tournament. The idea was seized upon with enthusiasm by the club and the inaugural Melrose Sevens was held at the Greenyards in April that year. The ladies of Melrose worked to raise funds for a trophy, which became known as the Ladies Cup. The trophy now sits in pride of place in the Ned Haig lounge at Melrose RFC.

In the years that have passed, the game has grown dramatically. Within ten years clubs all over the Borders and the North East of England were hosting their own sevens tournaments and in 1926 Twickenham hosted the inaugural Middlesex Sevens, which became one of the highlights of the season for nearly 70 years, until the advent of professionalism in 1995.

The spread of the game has been unrelenting. The Hong Kong Sevens was first staged in 1976 and has gone on to become a marquee event in the rugby calendar; in 1993 the first sevens World Cup was hosted at Murrayfield; and in 1999 the IRB launched the World Sevens Series, which has seen countries as diverse as China, Spain, Kenya, Russia and Portugal join the traditional rugby union powerhouse nations and the likes of Fiji, Samoa and the USA in competing for titles and trophies; the Commonwealth Games in 1998 in Kuala Lumpur featured sevens for the first time and the Olympics got in on the act by including sevens at the 2016 Rio Games after last featuring rugby in 1924. It is now a truly global sport and has a much greater reach than its incarnation as a 15-a-side game.

Some things never change, however, and the Ladies Cup is still contested at the Greenyards on the second Saturday of April every year and is a jewel in the Scottish rugby calendar. The players love it – and it is one hell of a party for spectators. Ned Haig was inducted into World Rugby's Hall of Fame in 2009.

15

Oh, Calcutta!

In 1878, the Calcutta Rugby Football Club, which had been formed in 1873, was dissolved due to a lack of support; the club members decided to melt down the last of their funds – a hoard of silver rupees – to create a cup that would be contested between Scotland and England. The cup was presented to the RFU by GAJ Rothney and was first contested in 1879. The match was drawn and so the first holder wasn't announced until the following year when England won at Whalley Range in Manchester. As of 2018, 125 Calcutta Cup matches have taken place, with England winning 70, Scotland 40 and with 15 matches drawn.

16

FAMOUS FIRSTS

Saturday is game day

The 1880 Home Nations match between Scotland and Ireland at Hamilton Crescent in Glasgow was the first Test match to be played on a Saturday, all the previous games having been played on a Monday. Scotland won by a goal, two drop-goals and two tries to nil after Edward Ewart scored a brace of tries and William Masters scored a try, one of which was converted by Malcolm Cross, while Ninian Finlay added two drop-goals.

17

FAMOUS FIRSTS

Scotland's first Lions skipper

Bill Maclagan became the first Scottish captain of the Lions in 1891 when he led the first touring team to visit South Africa. Born in Edinburgh, the piratical-looking Maclagan played his club rugby for London Scottish and won 26 caps for Scotland (1878-90), captaining his nation on eight occasions.

The 1891 Lions played 20 matches and won every one of them. Even more staggeringly, after conceding a score in the opening match in Cape Town, they didn't concede one again for the rest of the tour. Maclagan played in 18 of the 19 matches and scored eight tries. He was an ever-present as the Lions' inaugural Test series was won 3–0.

After retiring as a player, he served as SRU president from 1894-96 and died in 1926, aged 68. He was inducted into the World Rugby Hall of Fame in 2009

Scots everywhere

On the 1903 Lions tour to South Africa, Scotland provided the captains of both the Lions and the Springboks teams in the first Test of the series – and the referee. The match was played at Wanderers ground in Johannesburg; the Lions captain was Mark Morrison, who had first been capped as a teenager in 1896 and was later named as Scotland captain in 1899, a position that he held for 15 Tests through to 1904 – which included Triple Crown triumphs in 1901 and 1903.

A teammate of Morrison's from the 1901 Triple Crown winning side now stood opposite him as captain of the Springboks. Alex Frew had been born in Kilmarnock and trained to be a doctor at Edinburgh University before emigrating to Transvaal. He had won three caps for Scotland and this Test against the Lions would prove to be his only cap for his adopted country. He was joined in the Springbok side by Willie McEwan, who had won 16 caps for Scotland between 1894 and 1900 before also emigrating to South Africa, for whom he won two caps during the 1903 Test series with the Lions.

The man in the middle officiating the match was Bill Donaldson, who had represented Scotland himself, winning six caps between 1893 and 1899 and playing alongside Morrison and McEwan during several of these.

This game ended (rather appropriately) 10–all, with Frew scoring one of the tries. The second Test also ended in a draw, this time 0–0, before South Africa won the third Test 8–0 to take the series.

The best of the best

On the subject of the Lions, the following players have joined the exclusive ranks of those considered as the crème de la crème of the Home Unions with their selection for the combined touring team.

1888: AUSTRALIA and NEW ZEALAND
Five tourists: Herbert Brooks, Willie Burnet, Bob Burnet, Alex Laing, John Smith

1891: SOUTH AFRICA
Four tourists: Bill Maclagan (captain), Paul Clauss, Robert MacMillan, Willie Wotherspoon

1896: SOUTH AFRICA
No Scots selected

1899: AUSTRALIA
Two tourists: Alfred Bucher, Alec Timms

1903: SOUTH AFRICA
Seven tourists: David Bedell-Sivright, Louis Greig, John Gillespie, JC Hosack, Mark Morrison, Robert Neill, Bill Scott

1904: AUSTRALIA and NEW ZEALAND
One tourist: David Bedell-Sivright (captain)

1908: AUSTRALIA and NEW ZEALAND
No Scots selected (Scotland and Ireland declined to take part in the tour)

1910: SOUTH AFRICA
Six tourists: Eric Milroy, James Reid-Kerr, Dr W.A. Robertson, Louis Speirs, Robert Stevenson, Charles Timms

1910: ARGENTINA
Three tourists: Henry Fraser, William Fraser, Bertie Waddell

1924: SOUTH AFRICA
Ten tourists: Doug Davies, Dan Drysdale, Robert Henderson, Kelvin Hendrie, Bob Howie, Roy Kinnear, Neil Macpherson, Andrew Ross, Iain Smith, Herbert Waddell

1927: ARGENTINA
Four tourists: David MacMyn (captain), Peter Douty, Robert Kelly, Edward Taylor

1930: AUSTRALIA and NEW ZEALAND
One tourist: Willie Welsh

1936: ARGENTINA
Two tourists: Wilson Shaw, Jock Waters

1938: SOUTH AFRICA
Three tourists: Laurie Duff, Duncan Macrae, Jock Waters

1950: AUSTRALIA and NEW ZEALAND
Four tourists: Gus Black, Peter Kininmonth, Ranald Macdonald, Doug Smith

1955: SOUTH AFRICA
Six tourists: Angus Cameron, Tom Elliot, Jim Greenwood, Hughie McLeod, Ernie Michie, Arthur Smith

1959: AUSTRALIA and NEW ZEALAND
Five tourists: Stan Coughtrie, Hughie McLeod, Ken Scotland, Ken Smith, Gordon Waddell

1962: SOUTH AFRICA
Six tourists: Arthur Smith (captain), Mike Campbell-Lamerton, Ronnie Cowan, John Douglas, Dave Rollo, Gordon Waddell

1966: AUSTRALIA and NEW ZEALAND
Six tourists: Mike Campbell-Lamerton (captain), Derrick Grant, Sandy Hinshelwood, Frank Laidlaw, Jim Telfer, Stewart Wilson

1968: SOUTH AFRICA
Six tourists: Rodger Arneil, Gordon Connell, Sandy Hinshelwood, Peter Stagg, Jim Telfer, Jock Turner

1971: AUSTRALIA and NEW ZEALAND
Seven tourists: Rodger Arneil, Alastair Biggar, Gordon Brown, Sandy Carmichael, Frank Laidlaw, Ian McLauchlan, Chris Rea
Manager: Doug Smith

1974: SOUTH AFRICA
Six tourists: Gordon Brown, Sandy Carmichael, Andy Irvine, Ian McGeechan, Ian McLauchlan, Billy Steele

1977: NEW ZEALAND and FIJI
Five tourists: Gordon Brown, Bruce Hay, Andy Irvine, Ian McGeechan, Dougie Morgan

1980: SOUTH AFRICA
Five tourists: John Beattie, Bruce Hay, Andy Irvine, Jim Renwick, Alan Tomes

1983: NEW ZEALAND
Eight tourists: Roger Baird, John Beattie, Jim Calder, Colin Deans, Roy Laidlaw, Iain Milne, Iain Paxton, John Rutherford
Head coach: Jim Telfer

1989: AUSTRALIA
Nine tourists: Finlay Calder (captain), Gary Armstrong, Craig Chalmers, Peter Dods, Gavin Hastings, Scott Hastings, John Jeffrey, David Sole, Derek White
Head coach: Ian McGeechan

1993: NEW ZEALAND
Eight tourists: Gavin Hastings (captain), Paul Burnell, Damian Cronin, Scott Hastings, Kenny Milne, Andy Nicol, Andy Reed, Peter Wright
Head coach: Ian McGeechan

1997: SOUTH AFRICA
Six tourists: Tom Smith, Tony Stanger, Alan Tait, Gregor

Townsend, Rob Wainwright, Doddie Weir
Head coach: Ian McGeechan
Assistant coach: Jim Telfer

2001: AUSTRALIA
Five tourists: Gordon Bulloch, Scott Murray, Tom Smith, Simon Taylor, Andy Nicol (sat on the bench for the Third Test, but did not play on tour)

2005: NEW ZEALAND
Four tourists: Gordon Bulloch, Chris Cusiter, Simon Taylor, Jason White
Assistant coach: Ian McGeechan

2009: SOUTH AFRICA
Four tourists: Mike Blair, Ross Ford, Nathan Hines, Euan Murray
Head coach: Ian McGeechan

2013: AUSTRALIA
Four tourists: Ryan Grant, Richie Gray, Stuart Hogg, Sean Maitland
Manager: Andy Irvine

2017: NEW ZEALAND
Five tourists: Allan Dell, Stuart Hogg, Greig Laidlaw, Finn Russell, Tommy Seymour

The hard man

A year after Mark Morrison had led the Lions to South Africa, a teammate of his for both Scotland and the Lions took the reins for the 1904 Lions tour to Australia and New Zealand (becoming the only player to appear on both tours). David Bedell-Sivright made his international debut for Scotland at the age of 19 in 1900. He would establish a fearsome reputation and became widely regarded as the hardest man ever to have played for Scotland. He won four Blues while studying medicine at Cambridge and 22 caps for Scotland, during which time he earned the unique distinction of being the only Scot to have played in three Triple Crown winning sides (1901, 1903 and 1907).

Injury restricted him to just one cap for the 1904 Lions (the first Test against Australia), but he remained a guiding influence on the tour, which saw the Lions win all 14 of their matches in Australia, including the three Tests against the Wallabies.

The five-match New Zealand leg of the tour was less successful, however, with the Lions winning two provincial games, drawing one and losing one as well as falling to a 9–3 defeat to New Zealand in the single Test.

Bedell-Sivright settled in Sydney for a year after the tour before returning to Britain to complete his medical studies at Edinburgh University, whereupon he resumed his

Scotland career, captaining his country against the touring New Zealanders in 1905 and playing a significant part in the 6–0 defeat of the 1906 Springboks. He retired from Test rugby in 1908 and took up boxing, becoming Scotland's amateur boxing champion in 1909. Legends abound about Bedell-Sivright during his Edinburgh University days, from knocking out a cart horse with one punch after a heavy night of drinking, to lying prostrate across the tram tracks on Princes Street (after another heavy night on the sauce) and refusing to move, even when the police became involved – who were, it is alleged, too afraid to try to physically remove him themselves.

After the First World War broke out he was commissioned as a navy surgeon in January 1915 and in May was stationed at Gallipoli during the Dardanelles Campaign. After a period at a dressing station in the trenches, he was bitten by an insect. The bite became infected and he was taken offshore to the hospital ship HMHS *Dunluce Castle*. Two days later, on 5 September, he died of septicaemia – the mightiest of men felled by the smallest of creatures.

He was an inaugural inductee into the Scottish Rugby Hall of Fame in 2010, and in 2013 was inducted into the Rugby

21

STAT ZONE

Scotland's Home Nations record

The world's first international rugby union tournament (contested by Scotland, England, Ireland and Wales and known as the Home Unions Championship) was played from 1883 to 1909 before becoming the Five Nations in 1910 with the introduction of France. The tournament was resurrected between 1932 and 1939 when the French were temporarily expelled on the suspicion of professionalism among its players.

Championship wins: **10** (1887, 1889, 1891, 1895, 1901, 1903, 1904, 1907, 1933, 1938)

Championship wins (*shared title*): **3** (1886, shared with England; 1888, shared with England and Ireland; 1890, shared with England)

Triple Crowns: **7** (1891, 1895, 1901, 1903, 1907, 1933, 1938)

(IN)FAMOUS FIRSTS

Vive la France!
Viva l'Italia!

Scotland were the first team to lose to France in the Five
Nations, defeated 16–15 in Paris in 1911. Similarly, they
were the first team to be beaten by Italy in the expanded Six
Nations, losing 34–20 in Rome in 2000.

*Diego Dominguez hits a drop-goal during Italy's history-making
victory over Scotland in 2000.*

23

BLOOD ON THE THISTLE

The First World War

Scottish rugby players showed little hesitation in volunteering to serve King and country when the First World War broke out in August 1914. Consequently, the clubs were to pay a particularly heavy price for this heroism. Historians of the Gala, Hawick, Heriot's, Jed-forest and London Scottish clubs have reckoned that more than 750 of their club members signed up for active service, of whom nearly 200 were either killed in action or died of wounds before 1919 – a staggering attrition rate.

International players featured prominently among rugby's war-dead; of the 30 who had taken part in the Calcutta Cup match of March 1914, the last international played on British soil before the outbreak of war, 11 made the ultimate sacrifice. In all, 31 Scotland internationalists – more than any other rugby-playing country – were killed in action, listed as missing or died of wounds.

ROLL OF HONOUR 1914-1918

Abercrombie, Cecil Halliday (Scotland 1910-13) KIA when HMS *Defence* was blown up during the Battle of Jutland, 31 May 1916.

Bain, David McLaren (Scotland 1911-14) KIA at Festubert, France, 3 June 1915.

Bedell-Sivright, David Revell (Scotland 1900-08) Died of blood poisoning at Gallipoli, 5 September 1915.

Blair, Patrick Charles Bentley (Scotland 1912-13) KIA at Ypres, 6 July 1915.

Campbell, John Argentine (Scotland 1900) Died of wounds in Germany, 2 December, 1917.

Church, William Campbell (Scotland 1906) KIA at Gallipoli, 28 June 1915.

Dickson, Walter Michael ('Mike') (Scotland 1912-13) KIA at Loos, 26 September 1915.

Dods, John Henry (Scotland 1895-97) Killed on HMS *Natal* when it blew up at Cromarty, 30 December 1915.

Forrest, Walter Torrie (Scotland 1903-05) KIA at Gaza, 19 April 1917.

Fraser, Rowland (Scotland 1911) KIA on the Somme, 1 July 1916.

Gordon, Roland Elphinstone (Scotland 1913) Died of wounds, France, 30 August 1918.

Henderson, James Young Milne (Scotland 1911) KIA in Flanders, 31 July 1917.

Howie, David Dickie (Scotland 1912-13) Died of wounds, Gallipoli, 19 January 1916.

Huggan, James Laidlaw (Scotland 1914) KIA in the Battle of the Aisne, 16 September 1914.

Hutchison, William Ramsay (Scotland 1911) KIA at Arras, 22 March 1918.

Lamond, George Alexander Walker (Scotland 1899-1905) Died in Colombo from illness contracted in Mesopotamia, 25 February 1918.

Milroy, Eric (Scotland 1910-14) KIA on the Somme, 18 July 1916.

Nelson, Thomas Arthur (Scotland 1898) KIA at Arras, 9 April 1917.

Pearson, James (Scotland 1909-13) KIA at Hooge, Belgium, 22 May 1915.

Robertson, Lewis (Scotland 1908-13) Died of wounds at Ypres, 3 November 1914

Ross, Andrew (Scotland 1905-09) KIA in Flanders, 6 April 1916.

Ross, James (Scotland 1901-03) Missing presumed killed in action at Messines, October 31 1914.

Simson, Ronald Francis ('Ronnie') (Scotland 1911) KIA in the Battle of the Aisne, 14 September 1914.

Steyn, Stephen Sebastian Lombard ('Beak') (Scotland 1911-12) KIA in Palestine, 12 December 1917

Sutherland, Walter Riddell ('Wattie') (Scotland 1910-14) KIA at Hulluch, 4 October 1918.

Turner, Frederick Harding ('Freddie') (Scotland 1911-14) KIA near Kemmel, France, 10 January 1915.

Wade, Albert Luvian (Scotland 1908) KIA at Arras, 28 April 1917.

Wallace, William Middleton (Scotland 1913-14) Killed near Sainghin, France, 22 August 1915.

Will, John George (Scotland 1911-13) Missing presumed killed in action near Arras, 25 March 1917.

Wilson, John Skinner (Scotland 1908-09) KIA on HMS *Indefatigable* when she was sunk in the Battle of Jutland, 31 May 1916.

Young, Eric Templeton (Scotland 1914) KIA at Gallipoli, 28 June 1915.

Looking after the pennies

Jock Wemyss won two caps for Scotland as a prop in the 1914 Five Nations before the Great War put an end to international rugby for six years. He was injured on active service in the First World War and lost an eye. But despite this terrible injury, he returned to play for Scotland in 1920 for the first Five Nations match since the conflict – against France at the Stade Colombes in Paris on New Year's Day.

As the team sat in the changing room before the match, the baggage man began to hand out the jerseys – but he skipped Wemyss. When Wemyss enquired where his jersey was, he was told: 'You've already got one,' referring to the jersey he'd been given before the war, which he was expected to have brought along with him. When Wemyss explained that he had swapped the jersey with his opponent six years earlier, he was begrudgingly given a new one (but only after he had lined up topless in the tunnel before kick-off). He was subsequently issued with an invoice from the SRU for the swapped jersey.

There would be little change over the next 80 years when it came to the SRU and expenses. Some moments were comical – such as Frank Coutts being charged a penny to be weighed by an SRU official at a training session, or Peter Stagg having a public stand-off with the SRU secretary John Law over a *Playboy* magazine he had added to his expenses form (probably fair enough that Law challenged that one), or John Law being incensed that a selector had allowed John Frame to have lunch on SRU expenses on the day of a Test match (which was usually reserved for out-of-town players, not those based, like Frame, in Edinburgh).

Others were less amusing, however, such as the furore surrounding Budge Pountney's sudden retirement from Test rugby in 2003. Pountney had been engaged in an ongoing battle with the SRU over expenses and what he considered basic player-welfare at international training sessions. Pountney renounced the shambolic nature of the so-called professional environment, citing a lack of water and food at training, an inability to get basic items of kit such as spare studs, and he raised the issue of an invoice that he had been constantly reissued with for a tie he'd given away to a young fan. Pountney was undoubtedly justified in his ire and the whole episode was an embarrassment to Scottish rugby, but when compared to the treatment of the war hero, Wemyss, it pales in significance to what was surely the SRU's penny-pinching nadir.

'I get hungry when I'm bored'

There can't be many players who have taken to the field so pessimistic about their chances of seeing the ball that they brought their own snacks with them to help stave off the boredom – but that's exactly what happened (allegedly) during Scotland's 1923 match against France at Inverleith when one of the French wings, who hadn't had a sniff of any action, pulled an apple from his pocket and began to eat it. Scotland, perhaps unsurprisingly, won the match 16–3 – with two tries from centre Teddy McLaren, one from scrum-half Willie Bryce and one from winger Eric Liddell who, one can only presume, had little difficulty getting around his pomme-crunching opposite number.

Man on a mission

Eric Liddell was born in January 1902 in Tientsin (now Tianjin) in northern China, while his parents were working as missionaries for the London Missionary Society.

He was educated in the UK at Eltham College in Blackheath before following his brother, Rob, to Edinburgh University, where he read for a BSc in Pure Science. Away from his studies, both religion and sport dominated his life. He ran in the 100 yards and the 220 yards for the university athletics team and later for Scotland, and also played rugby for the university. In 1922 he was selected on the wing for his Test debut against France at Colombes. The match, played on a heavy pitch on 2 January, ended in a 3–3 draw, and his second cap against Wales at Inverleith also ended in a draw, this time 9–9. It took a while for him to settle into Test rugby, but when he did his electric pace proved devastating. He scored in his third Test, a victory over Ireland in Edinburgh, and again a year later in his fourth cap, a thumping 16–3 victory over France. Most famously, however, he scored a searing try against Wales in 1923, to help secure the first Scottish victory in Cardiff for 33 years. He won seven caps in total, losing just once (to England in his final Test) and scoring four tries, before taking the decision to drop out of rugby to focus on athletics ahead of the 1924 Olympic Games in Paris – which were immortalised in the movie *Chariots of Fire*. It was here that his legend was established for ever. Considered a strong favourite to take gold in the 100 metres, his preferred distance, he learned that the heats were to be run on a Sunday. His religious beliefs prevented him from running on the Sabbath, so he switched to the 400 metres – and won gold. He also picked up a bronze medal in the 200 metres.

At the conclusion to the Olympics, he returned to Edinburgh to complete his degree and after returning to China to work as a missionary, he was ordained as a minister in 1932. After the outbreak of the Second World War his travels around China regularly took him across Japanese military lines and, despite warnings from the Foreign Office to return home, he continued his work – until he was captured by the Japanese in 1943 and interred in a prisoner of war camp in Weihsien (now Weifang). Tragically, he developed a brain tumour while in the camp and, his condition no doubt worsened by malnourishment and overwork, he succumbed to the disease on 21 February 1945, five months before the camp was liberated by Allied forces.

Considered one of the greatest sportsmen ever produced by Scotland, he was inducted into the Scottish Sports Hall of Fame in 2002.

27

What a way to open the Big House

Murrayfield Stadium was opened in 1925 and Scotland marked the occasion in the most spectacular of styles when they won their first Grand Slam.

The first match of that year's Five Nations was played at Inverleith as Murrayfield wasn't ready yet, and Scotland won 25–4 with wing Ian Smith scoring four tries to go with a brace for Johnnie Wallace on the opposite flank and a try by back-rower Sandy Gillies.

A fortnight later they travelled to Swansea to play Wales and Smith again scored four tries, taking his tally to a remarkable eight tries after just two rounds of the competition. Scotland emerged 24–14 winners thanks to Smith's efforts and another two tries for Wallace allied to the reliable boot of full-back Dan Drysdale.

The match against Ireland in Dublin was a much tighter affair. Johnnie Wallace was on the scoresheet for the third game in a row, with second-row David MacMyn also crossing. Drysdale and centre Jimmy Dykes added conversions and fly-half Herbert Waddell slotted a drop-goal to secure a 14–8 victory.

The decider against England was the first game to be played at the new home of Scottish rugby. England had beaten Wales and drawn with Ireland (both games were at Twickenham) and would go on to defeat France at Colombes three weeks later. The visitors, led by the great William Wavell Wakefield, had been the best side in the Championship since the Great War and had won Grand Slams in 1921, 1923 and 1924 (to go with the two they had won immediately before the war in 1913 and 1914). Both sides scored a brace of tries in the opening hour and as the game moved into the final quarter, England were ahead 11–10 thanks to a William Luddington penalty. It was Waddell, however, who claimed the victory for his side with a drop-goal from 25 yards out that sent the crowd into raptures and his team into the history books.

Scotland's 1925 Grand Slam team before the England game.

28

Number the cattle

It took 57 years of Test rugby before Scotland wore numbers on their jerseys, and that was long after the other major nations began doing so. The delay in taking up the practice was due in large part to the fierce resistance to the idea from SRU secretary J. Aikman Smith, who abhorred the concept. Aikman Smith eventually relented and Scotland wore numbers on their jerseys for the first time in Paris in 1928. This practice was only experimental, however, and Aikman Smith abolished it again until the Welsh match of 1933 at Swansea, whereafter they wore them permanently. Aikman Smith had been questioned about the lack of numbers by King George V during the 1926 Calcutta Cup at Twickenham. Smith had responded to His Majesty's query by declaring, 'it is a rugby match not a cattle sale', and the SRU managed, rather admirably, to hold out against the tide of change for another seven years.

29

FAMOUS FIRSTS

Rugby on TV

1938 saw the BBC televise its first ever live Test match – the Calcutta Cup encounter at Twickenham on 19 March – although it could only be enjoyed by those who lived within 20 miles of London. Scotland won 21–16 to secure the Triple Crown. Scottish captain and fly-half Wilson Shaw was at his swashbuckling best during the match, revelling in the dry conditions on a sunny March day to score two rip-roaring tries. He was supported by a skilful three-quarter line in Duncan Macrae and Charles Dick (who also scored a try) in midfield and John Forrest and Bill Renwick (who, like Shaw, scored two tries) on the wing.

30

BLOOD ON THE THISTLE

The Second World War

There was no shortage of volunteers from the Scottish rugby community when, for the second time in barely a quarter of a century, the call to arms to serve King and country came in September 1939 and the Five Nations Championship slipped into hibernation during the Second World War. Murrayfield was converted into a supply depot for the Royal Army Service Corps and, until 1944 when it was derequisitioned and the home tie in the annual Scotland versus England services internationals was played, the turnstiles lay still. Between 1942 and 1945 the armed services played these games over two legs, home and away, and before the return to Murrayfield in 1944, the first two home matches were staged at Inverleith.

In all, eight internationals took place across the four war-torn seasons, England winning five to Scotland's three. With many top-class rugby players from the Commonwealth stationed across the United Kingdom, qualification rules were relaxed. Thus Ronald Rankin, an Australian Test full-back, could turn out in an English jersey against the Scots at

Wembley in 1942 and Rod McKenzie, who had locked the scrum for the All Blacks against Scotland at Murrayfield in 1935, was in blue for the last two games of the series in 1945. The matches provided important practice for seasoned players and helped many younger ones establish their credentials as potential post-war internationalists. The fixtures, moreover, proved welcome diversions from the everyday tensions of the war for the thousands of spectators who turned out to watch them.

Although the toll was not as great as it was in the First World War, Scotland lost a generation of players to the Second, with 14 capped internationalists alone killed in action, nearly half of them while serving in the RAF.

ROLL OF HONOUR 1939-1945

Dorward, Thomas Fairgrieve (Scotland 1938-39) Died of wounds in Castle Bytham, Lincolnshire on 5 March 1941.

Forrest, John Gordon Scott (Scotland 1938) Killed in an aircraft crash on 14 September 1942.

Gallie, George Holmes (Scotland 1939) KIA at Minturno, Italy, on 16 January 1944.

Kinnear, Roy Muir (Scotland 1926) Died playing in a Service match at Uxbridge on 22 September 1942.

Liddell, Eric Henry (Scotland 1922-23) Died in a PoW camp at Weihsien, Shantung province, China on 21 February 1945.

MacKenzie, Donald Kenneth Andrew (Scotland 1939) Killed in a training flight crash south of Edinburgh on 12 June 1940.

McNeil, Alastair Simpson Bell (Scotland 1935) KIA at Anzio, Italy on 26 January 1944.

Munro, Patrick (Scotland 1905-11) Killed on Home Guard duty in Westminster on 3 May 1942.

Penman, William Mitchell (Scotland 1939) Died when his Lancaster went missing on a raid over Kassel, Germany on 3 October 1943.

Renwick, William Norman (Scotland 1938-39) KIA at Bolsena in Italy, on 15 June 1944.

Ritchie, James McPhail (Scotland 1933-34) Died of fever in Rawalpindi on 6 July 1942.

Roberts, George (Scotland 1938-39) Died as a PoW of the Japanese on 2 August 1943.

Ross, William Alexander (Scotland 1937) Died serving as a pilot in North Africa, on 28 September 1941.

St Clair-Ford, Drummond (Scotland 1930-32) Missing presumed drowned after the submarine *Traveller* was lost in the Gulf of Taranto on 12 December 1942.

FAMOUS FIRSTS

When we beat New Zealand

Now we all know the stats, don't we? Scotland have never beaten the All Blacks.

Except for the time we did.

When the Second World War ended, international rugby resumed with a series of Victory Internationals held in the 1945–46 season among the Home Nations and the touring New Zealand Army side – the so-called Kiwis or 'Khaki All Blacks'. The tourists wore the traditional black strip with the silver fern and were captained by pre-war All Black Charlie Saxton. The team was filled with All Blacks and also several New Zealand rugby league players. Scotland back-row John Orr remarked that the side were actually *better* than the All Blacks with the inclusion of the professional league players.

The Kiwis played 33 matches on a European tour that lasted from late-October 1945 until the end of March 1946, losing only twice: against Monmouthshire at Pontypool and to Scotland in a thrilling match at Murrayfield in mid-January.

Ian Geddes led Scotland, all in white, from full-back and his side came from behind in the second half to lead 8–6 with time running out. Ian Lumsden and Russell Bruce had combined to send John Anderson over in the corner before Bill Munro scored and Doug Smith added the conversion. In a tense finish, Anderson, a real flyer on the right wing, sealed Scotland's first (and only) victory over a New Zealand representative team to date by sprinting to the corner to touch down after Bruce had fired wide with a drop-goal attempt.

Just remember this result the next time Scotland face the All Blacks and the pundits say we've never beaten them, OK? (Even if it wasn't an official Test . . .)

Action from the 1946 Victory International against New Zealand.

FAMOUS FIRSTS

Scotland's first matches against international opposition

The first time that Scotland faced-off against their traditional international rivals was as follows:

v England, 1871 (won 1G 1T to 1T)
v Ireland, 1877 (won 4G 2DG 2T to nil)
v Wales, 1883 (won 3G to 1G)
v New Zealand, 1905 (lost 12–7)
v South Africa, 1906 (won 6–0)
v France, 1910 (won 27–0)
v Australia, 1927 (won 10–8)

Although Scotland had played several of the following countries before the dates given below, these were the first encounters to be awarded official Test status by the SRU (unlike other international sports, it's the Unions themselves who award matches Test status):

v Romania, 1981 (won12–6)
v Zimbabwe, 1987 (won 60–21)
v Fiji, 1989 (won 38–17)
v Argentina, 1990 (won 49–3)
v Japan, 1991 (won 47–9)
v Western Samoa, 1991 (won 28–6)

v Canada, 1995 (won 22–6)
v Ivory Coast, 1995 (won 89–0)
v Tonga, 1995 (won 41–5)
v Italy, 1996 (won 29–22)
v Uruguay, 1999 (won 43–12)
v Spain, 1999 (won 48–0)
v United States, 2000 (won 53–6)
v Pacific Islands, 2006 (won 34–22)
v Portugal, 2007 (won 56–10)
v Georgia, 2011 (won 15–6)

'Oh good, another line-out'

The match against Wales during the 1963 Five Nations slipped into rugby folklore not for impressive attacking flair or spectacular tries, nor even for blood and guts defence or shocking violence, but because of the tactics adopted by Welsh captain Clive Rowlands. The scrum-half led his side out at Murrayfield and orchestrated a game plan that looked almost exclusively to take advantage of the law that allowed the ball to be kicked out on the full from any area of the field and would see a line-out take place where the ball crossed the line. As a result, there were 111 line-outs during the game.

As George Stevenson later recalled: 'That was one of the first times I played on the wing for Scotland and in those days the winger threw the ball in at the line-out. I touched the ball more that day than I ever touched it in any match before or since, but it was only to throw the ball in after Rowlands had kicked to touch again. Wales won 6–0. What a dreadful game. They changed the rules after that, making it illegal to kick direct to touch unless you were in your own 22.'

FAMOUS FIRSTS

The world's first national league

Until the 1973/74 season, Scottish clubs had played in what had become known as the 'unofficial championship', a network of fixtures between clubs that provided an unofficial champion each year and a rough league table, but which contained various anomalies (such as some clubs playing fewer fixtures than others or some playing against weaker opposition than others). In 1973, however, the SRU organised its full member clubs into six leagues, giving an official structure to the season that didn't, at the time, exist anywhere else in the world. Hawick were the first official national champions and went on to dominate the early years of the league which, to date, they have won 12 times.

35

Have boots, will (eventually) travel

Scotland's first overseas tour was to South Africa in 1960. Although the Lions had been touring since 1888, this sojourn to South Africa was the first overseas tour undertaken by one of the individual four Home Unions – coming 55 years after the All Blacks (in 1905), 54 years after the Springboks (in 1906) and 52 years after the Wallabies (in 1908) had toured the UK for the first time.

36

FAMOUS FIRSTS
Fresh legs

Scrum-half Iain McCrae of Gordonians became the first player to come on as a substitute in a Five Nations Test match when he replaced Gordon Connell against France in Paris in 1969. Despite being outplayed for much of the match, Scotland went on to win the game 6–3. McCrae won a total of six caps and enjoyed a long club career, playing for Gordonians in four decades from 1959 to 1981.

37

The toughest of tours

Scotland toured Argentina in the summer of 1969, playing four provincial games and two matches against the Pumas. These latter two weren't awarded Test status as the IRB didn't allow member unions to award caps against countries who were then outside board membership – as Argentina were at the time – until 1981.

Jim Telfer believes that the demands of the tour brought a hardness to the Scottish forward game that went through the seventies and contributed in no small part to the success of the victorious Lions tours to New Zealand in 1971 and to South Africa in 1974 where the likes of Ian McLauchlan and Sandy Carmichael were key to the Lions' forward dominance. 'When people ask me what was the hardest tour I ever went on,' said Telfer, 'I always tell them it was that trip to Argentina, without any question of a doubt.

'We won all the provincial matches but in the first game against the national side we lost Ian Murchie in the opening minutes when he was short-armed by a guy called Alessandro Travaglini and we had to play with 14 players – because it wasn't a cap international we weren't allowed substitutions – and we lost 20–3. I had never seen grown men cry after a game until that tour.

'We then went to Rosario for the second Test and there were these national strikes going on. We had to walk to the game in twos and threes because the buses had been commandeered by the strikers and they were burning them. Before we left for the match, we went up on to the hotel roof in Rosario and we were looking around pointing out fires to each other – it was the buses being burned. This was before the game. The atmosphere was very hostile.

'We decided in the forwards that if one of our guys got hit we were all going to go in to make sure we were never second best – and they couldn't send off eight forwards.'

'Being in Argentina was the closest I've ever been to a war,' recalled Sandy Carmichael. 'Things were crazy out on the streets – and pretty crazy out on the field as well. One game had to be postponed for two days due to snipers, which was a first.'

'Our full-back, Colin Blaikie, would take all our place-kicks and he had to try and do it while the crowd threw coins at him,' said Telfer. 'They were bouncing all around him and ricocheting off his head and arms and legs. It was unbelievable, a real bear pit.'

'On the day of the match they had women with live pumas on chains on the pitch before the game,' remembered Norman Suddon, who was watching from the stands. 'It was a culture shock – really hostile. But Creamy [Jim Telfer], the captain, took control. He got the players through into a room by themselves and he said that it was going to be one for all and all for one. At the first scrum it was a case of hit anything within range – and we won the match in the end. All because Creamy decided we were going to fight fire with fire. I take my hat off to him, he turned it around.'

'We came back from Argentina and in our next match beat

South Africa 6–3 at Murrayfield, which was pretty special,' said McLauchlan. 'A lot of the success we enjoyed throughout the seventies, particularly with the Lions, came from our experiences in Argentina. It was a tough tour but it was the making of us.'

Beating England twice in a week

1971 saw the centenary anniversary of the (English) Rugby Football Union. As part of the celebrations, two Calcutta Cup matches were scheduled during that year's Five Nations (with only the first match, at Twickenham, counting towards the Championship, before a return 'friendly' at Murrayfield the following week). Scotland secured their first win at Twickenham in 33 years in the first fixture, winning 16–15, before backing up this triumph seven days later with a thumping 26–6 win at home. The 1971 team remains the only Scotland side to have beaten England twice in a single season.

The teams pose together for the Centenary Match photograph

STAT ZONE

Record crowd at Murrayfield

Although it is impossible to record the exact number who attended this game, it is estimated (and widely accepted) that as many as 104,000 spectators flooded into Murrayfield to watch Scotland play Wales during the 1975 Five Nations. Scotland won 12–10 thanks to an Ian McGeechan drop-goal and three penalties from Dougie Morgan.

Black out

In the autumn of 1983, just months after the All Blacks had dismantled the Lions 4–0 in that summer's Test series, Scotland welcomed New Zealand to Murrayfield. In what was to prove a heroic display, albeit heart-wrenching that they weren't able to complete the job, Scotland drew 25–25 with their exalted visitors. The match itself has had very little exposure, however, as a TV technicians' strike meant that the game wasn't televised in the UK and any of the Scotland players who wanted to get hold of a recording had to try to lay their hands on a recording of the coverage that was beamed to New Zealand.

All Black flanker Jock Hobbs scored a try and winger Bernie Fraser scored two while Robbie Deans added two conversions and three penalties; Scotland's points came from two John Rutherford drop-goals and five Peter Dods penalties, to leave Scotland trailing 25–21 going into the final minutes.

With one last play of the game left, Scotland were awarded a line-out. Bill Cuthbertson won the ball and Rutherford spun it out to centre David Johnston, who chipped a delicate kick over the onrushing All Blacks defence for Jim Pollock to score in the corner. Full-back Dods had a kick from the right-hand side-line to win the game, but he pushed it wide and both sides had to settle for an honourable draw.

41

The second Slammers

After the inaugural Home Unions Championship in 1883 (which became the Five Nations in 1910), it had taken Scotland until 1925 to complete a clean sweep and claim their first Grand Slam. It took them another 59 years to win their second.

Coming into the 1984 Five Nations, Scotland had recorded a 25–25 draw with the All Blacks at Murrayfield in November 1983, just months after the Kiwis had eviscerated the Lions 4–0 in the Test series that summer. A core of eight Scotland players, plus coach Jim Telfer, had returned from the Lions tour chastened by the experience but also determined to use the lessons they had learned to advance the Scottish cause in the Five Nations. They opened their campaign in Cardiff, a feeling of confidence in their step after victory at the Arms Park in 1982, which had been their first in Wales for 20 years. Captain Jim Aitken and number eight Iain Paxton both scored tries and the dead-eyed kicking of full-back Peter Dods helped secure a 15–9 victory and a priceless start to the Championship.

The Calcutta Cup at Murrayfield was the hundredth game between Scotland and England and the visitors came into the match on the back of a great win over New Zealand in the autumn. It was the classic clash of the English maul versus the Scottish ruck and on the day it was the ruck that won out.

There was a month between the Calcutta Cup and the next fixture against Ireland. Scotland travelled to Dublin in search of their first Triple Crown since 1938 and they came up against a side that had shared the Championship with France the previous year but had lost to both Wales and England. Scotland ran riot, scoring five tries on their way to a thumping 32–9 victory. With the Triple Crown secured, all eyes turned to the final match against France at Murrayfield.

The French had been racking up high scores of their own, defeating Ireland 25–12 at the Parc des Princes, Wales 21–16 in Cardiff, and England 32–18 at the Parc. The visitors flew out of the blocks and completely outplayed Scotland in the first half and were leading 12–9 midway through the second half. But then back-row David Leslie put in a devastating tackle on Jerome Gallion that saw the influential French scrum-half injured out of the game. It was a turning point.

SCOTLAND 12 FRANCE 12 ☒ The Royal Bank 16

Jim Calder's try pushes Scotland into the lead against France.

42

FAMOUS FIRSTS

Scotland's first World Cup match

After years of wrangling between the world's major rugby nations, the IRB finally announced that they would hold a World Cup tournament in 1987. Sixteen nations would contest for the Webb Ellis Cup at the inaugural Rugby World Cup, which was co-hosted by New Zealand and Australia between 22 May and 20 June that year.

Scotland's prospects were marred before the tournament even began thanks to career-ending injuries to two of their most influential players. Number eight John Beattie ruptured his knee ligaments in the Calcutta Cup and was forced into retirement and then, just a couple of weeks before the squad was due to fly to New Zealand, fly-half John Rutherford also injured his knee playing in an exhibition game in Bermuda. Rutherford hoped he could get his knee in shape for the tournament but he lasted just 15 minutes of the first match and was never to play for Scotland again.

That first match in Scotland's World Cup adventure was against France at Lancaster Park in Christchurch on 23 May. It was widely accepted that the clash would decide the outcome of Pool 4 as the other nations grouped with Scotland and

France were Zimbabwe and Romania. Despite the early loss of Rutherford, Scotland moved into a 13–6 lead at half-time. But second-half scores from Philippe Sella and Serge Blanco pushed France into the lead until Matt Duncan slashed down the wing in injury time to draw the match 20–20. Gavin Hastings had a kick from the touchline to win the game, but the angle, the distance and the Christchurch wind conspired against him and the ball slid wide. Despite the match being drawn, France were handed the initiative in the pool as they had outscored Scotland in the try count.

Both Scotland and France strolled to wins in their remaining pool matches – 60–21 against Zimbabwe and 55–28 against Romania in Scotland's case – and the result in Christchurch pushed Scotland into a quarter-final with the eventual champions, New Zealand. They were swept aside by tries from full-back John Gallagher and lock Gary Whetton, both of which were converted by Grant Fox. Along with six Fox penalties, the match finished 30–3 and ended Scotland's participation in the tournament.

One twin for another

It is an extraordinary fact that twin brothers Jim and Finlay Calder won Grand Slams for their country and toured with the Lions to establish their legend as two of the greatest back-row forwards to ever play for Scotland and the Lions –

but they never played together for either team. Jim was the pace-setter, breaking into the Scotland team in 1981 and touring with the 1983 Lions before sealing the 1984 Grand Slam with a try against France. He played his final Test in 1985 and was then replaced in the team by his twin, who won the first of his 37 caps in 1986 before captaining the Lions to a series victory over Australia in 1989, winning a Grand Slam of his own in 1990 and then retiring after the 1991 World Cup.

'I think I blossomed as a player earlier than Fin because I had it in my mind from a young age that that was what I wanted to do,' explains Jim. 'I remember going to watch a Scotland trial when I was about eight-years-old and just sitting there spellbound by the whole thing. It just got into my blood and into my system at an early age that this was what I wanted to do with my life. But it didn't hit Fin like that. He was just a different character. We had a field alongside our house and I would spend hours there kicking a ball about, while he would be off at our cousins' farm driving tractors and so on. That drive to succeed in rugby didn't kick in until a wee bit later.

'And I probably didn't help because as a youngster I was always trying to keep him in his cage. I think I was naturally more competitive and I think I still am, but there is a hardness to Fin which was most evident when he was on the pitch and all countries recognised and respected that – which is completely at odds to this gentle character you see off the field.

'A defining moment in Fin's career was this horrible, wet, windy November evening in the mid-eighties when we had gone out to train together. We were running round the perimeter of the Riccarton campus in Edinburgh and no matter what direction we were going the wind seemed to be in our faces. About halfway round I'm thinking, "this is really hard work but I have to keep plugging away", so I push on a bit and get into the changing room.

'Eventually Fin stumbled in and I said to him, "you're f***ing useless. It was hard for me as well, but you just gave up."

'It was like a light-bulb came on above his head. He said: "Was it? Was it really tough for you?"

'We did the same run a week later, and at about the same spot he just took off, and he never looked back. It goes back to him having less confidence, for whatever reason – like having a sneaky twin brother undermining him – but it eventually dawned on him that he could do it, and then Jim Telfer gave him a bit more confidence as his coach, and all of a sudden he was captain of the Lions and this incredibly important player in a great Scotland team. Because he had pace and that in-built hardness on the pitch, he found it remarkably easy to step up once he had switched on to what he was capable of.'

44

Sing it loud, sing it proud

Perhaps the most famous rendition of *Flower of Scotland* occurred before the 1990 Grand Slam showdown against England at Murrayfield, but that game is often incorrectly cited as the first time the song was played as Scotland's national anthem before a rugby Test match. It was, in fact, first sung the previous autumn, and had been established as an unofficial anthem as early as 1974.

Tony Stanger (Scotland 1989-98, 52 caps): I won my first cap against Fiji in 1989, which was obviously a very memorable game for me as it was my first game and I scored two tries, but it was also momentous because it was the first time that *Flower of Scotland* was played as our national anthem before a game. It used to be *God Save the Queen*, but it was changed that year and *Flower of Scotland* has been our anthem ever since.

Ian McGeechan (Scotland 1972-79, 40 caps): Billy Steele brought *Flower of Scotland* to rugby. It became the tour song on the '74 Lions tour. We sung it before every game and every Test match and it was the last thing we would sing before we got off the bus – and we wouldn't get off the bus until we'd finished it. And we then sang it live on television after the tour and gradually the players in Scotland began to sing it themselves on the field until it became the thing that we sung before the matches at Murrayfield. I can still remember the first time it was sung before an international and I realised how far it had come. I remember it being sung and thinking about Billy and how he had started all that – and it was a very powerful, emotional song that a lot of people had shared, not just Scots.

45

The Grandest of Slams

After leading the Lions to a Test series victory over Australia in 1989, head coach Ian McGeechan and captain Finlay Calder returned to the Scotland squad with their minds spinning into overdrive ahead of the 1990 Five Nations. The key personnel in the Lions' series victory had, by and large, been English, despite key input from the likes of Gavin and Scott Hastings, David Sole and Calder. England would present a mighty challenge in time, but McGeechan knew he had some special players of his own coming together north of the border.

Towards the end of 1988, a group of senior players had travelled down to Selkirk for a meeting with Jim Telfer to persuade the coach out of retirement. The ploy worked and by the end of 1989 the silver-haired taskmaster was back to harangue, berate, abuse and improve the Scottish pack as only he knew how.

Having sat out the first round of matches of the 1990 Championship, which had seen England dismantle Ireland 23–0 at Twickenham, Scotland started their campaign with something of a whimper by comparison, scraping past a limited Irish side 13–10 at Lansdowne Road. The visitors were 7–0 down at half-time before Derek White stole the show with two tries, the first of which was converted by Craig Chalmers.

It hadn't been a result to set the world alight, but a win on the road was invaluable. As the players were getting showered, however, news started to filter in from Paris where England were playing France at the Parc des Princes; or, to be more accurate, obliterating France at the Parc des Princes. In one of the fiercest rugby environments on the planet, Will Carling's team won 26–7, scoring three tries, four penalties and a conversion in the process. It was a monumental result.

Scotland faced France at Murrayfield in the next round and knew that they would be facing a wounded beast. The French players would come at Scotland with all guns blazing; the question was whether they would be able to conjure a response to the England result, or whether the psychological damage of that game had left them vulnerable.

French coach Jacques Fouroux made sweeping changes to his side, dropping captain Pierre Berbizier and handing the armband to Laurent Rodriguez, known as the Dax Bull, and picking the gigantic Alain Carminati on the openside flank.

Scotland had a poor first half and despite playing with a strong wind at their backs, went in at half-time just 3–0 ahead. But then two things fell in their favour. First, the wind changed – almost at the moment the players emerged back on to the field – and was, once again, at Scotland's back. Then there was a moment of madness from Carminati. John Jeffrey, in a characteristic moment of skulduggery, grabbed hold of a French leg while he was lying at the bottom of a ruck. It was Carminati's – and the Frenchman wasn't pleased. He kicked out at JJ and caught him in the head. Referee Fred Howard was on the spot and had little option but to send Carminati to the stands. French heads dropped and the Scots put their foot down. They scored tries through Calder and winger Iwan

Tukalo and the boot of Gavin Hastings and Chalmers did the rest as they pushed on for a 21–0 victory.

Scotland headed down to Cardiff for their third game and were prepared, once again, for a backlash from their opposition. While Scotland had been seeing off France, Wales had been thumped 34–6 at Twickenham and in the aftermath of that game their coach, John Ryan, had quit. He was replaced at the helm by Ron Waldron, the head coach at Neath, who played a fast, loose game with athletic forwards, very much like Scotland. But it was here that Telfer's nous and experience came to the fore. He knew that the key ingredient to fielding a quick forward pack was that there still needed to be a balance to its make-up; you can't have a pack of eight whippets – you also need ballast. In tight-head Paul Burnell and second-row Damian Cronin, Scotland had that ballast, while Waldron went lightweight everywhere. Scotland destroyed them in the scrums and the only disappointment from a Scottish point of view was that they didn't make that dominance translate on the scoreboard. Nevertheless, they secured victory, 13–9, with

Finlay Calder bursts into space against Ireland.

Cronin crashing over to score and Chalmers knocking over three penalties.

'It was a very strange year,' recalled Gavin Hastings. 'We went over to Dublin first up and sneaked a win, then came back to Scotland and beat a 14-man France team fairly handsomely after Alain Carminati was sent off, then went to Wales and won. So we weren't playing particularly great rugby, but we were winning our games and all of a sudden we were going into the last weekend with three wins and a real chance of a Grand Slam. It just kind of crept up on us.'

And so it came down to one game. Winner takes all.

McGeechan, Telfer and their assistants Dougie Morgan and Derrick Grant pored over video tapes as they tried to find a way to counter the awesome power of the England pack and their electric backs, who had been racking up points for fun throughout the Championship. They had scored 11 tries and conceded only two. Scotland had scored five and also conceded just two but in none of their victories had they displayed the dominance that England had shown in the previous rounds.

The Championship, the Triple Crown, the Calcutta Cup and the Grand Slam were now up for grabs and as far as anybody outside the Scotland dressing room could see, they were England's for the taking.

Anti-Englishness and, in particular, anti-Thatcherism swirled around Scotland in the build-up to the match, ramped up to near incendiary levels by the national press. This was fuelled in large part by the opposition across Scotland to Thatcher's poll tax experiment, which she had launched in Scotland in 1989 as a trial before it was rolled out across the rest of the UK, and in part because there was now a vacuum in the sporting calendar as the annual Scotland-England football fixture had been cancelled after years of escalating hooliganism around the match. The Calcutta Cup now filled this vacuum.

England's rugby team, and their captain Will Carling in particular, were portrayed as Thatcher's representatives on the sporting field. Which was a ridiculous tarnishing, especially as members of the England team, such as hooker Brian Moore, were as vocally opposed to the poll tax as the Scots themselves.

But the press and the public lapped up the ill-feeling as the match approached and everything from Bannockburn to Flodden was trotted out as the home team prepared to welcome the English to Murrayfield.

England ran out to a mixture of cheers and boos, a stiff wind blowing and the sun peeking occasionally from behind clouds. The pitch was dry and fast; they were, as Bill McLaren commented at that very moment, near-perfect rugby conditions. Then came Sole and his team – walking out of the tunnel. The ground around Murrayfield trembled with the roar of the crowd. McLaren, the fairest and most unbiased of commentators, was momentarily lost for words with the emotion of the occasion.

David Sole marches his men out for the Grand Slam decider.

It was an epic match, one that fully deserves its place in the pantheon of great sporting conflicts, full of ebbs and flows and dozens of minor battles that were won and lost in almost equal measure by both sides. Almost equal.

Scotland went ahead with two early penalties nudged over by Chalmers before England struck back with the kind of attacking élan they'd been showing all season. From a scrum the ball went wide, Carling shimmied and stood up the defence, creating space outside him. Guscott flew on to the ball and, with the defence drifting to cover the overlap outside him, he dummied and glided in to score – his seventh try for England in just six Tests. The conversion was missed and Scotland held on to their lead, 6–4, before pushing further ahead before half-time with another Chalmers penalty.

Then, early in the second half, came one of the most famous scoring passages in Scottish sport. Derek White had gone off injured, so Jeffrey packed down at number eight at a scrum just inside the English half. He picked up and broke down the blindside, slipped the ball to Gary Armstrong, who drew the covering tackles of Mike Teague and Rob Andrew before releasing Gavin Hastings down the wing. Hastings juggled the ball, fixed Rory Underwood and then chipped the ball ahead just as he was being bundled into touch. Twenty-one-year-old winger Tony Stanger hared after the ball and used his height advantage to just get to it before Underwood to touch down in the corner. Scotland were unable to convert, but Chalmers and England full-back Simon Hodgkinson added a penalty each to take the score to 13–7, which was how the game ended. The Calcutta Cup, Triple Crown, Five Nations Championship and the Grand Slam were Scotland's. Glory days.

46

FAMOUS FIRSTS

The full house

Craig Chalmers became the first Scotland player to complete the 'full house' of scoring in every possible way in a single match when Scotland played Wales at Murrayfield during the 1991 Five Nations. Having lost to France in Paris in the opening round of the Championship, Scotland bounced back with a decisive 32–12 victory over Wales in which Chalmers scored a try, a conversion, a penalty and a drop-goal to go alongside tries from Gary Armstrong and a brace from Derek White, and a conversion and two penalties from Gavin Hastings.

Craig Chalmers gets his backline moving against Wales in 1991.

47

A game of inches

A year after the heroics of the 1990 Grand Slam, England well and truly got their revenge over their old enemy. They picked up a Grand Slam of their own (the first of two back-to-back Grand Slam campaigns), which included a comprehensive 21–12 victory over Scotland at Twickenham.

Then, that autumn, came the World Cup – which was jointly hosted by Scotland, England, Ireland, Wales and France.

Scotland were pooled with Japan, Zimbabwe and Ireland. The first two were dispatched with ease, 47–9 and 51–12, before the crunch encounter against Ireland at Murrayfield. It was a tight affar for much of the match, but the game turned in Scotland's favour when Ireland's Jim Staples fielded a high ball from Craig Chalmers and was flattened by Finlay Calder just as he caught it. A few minutes later Chalmers put up another high ball on a visibly shaken Staples, who fluffed his catch. The ball ricocheted off his shoulder and straight into centre Graham Shiel's arms, and he scored under the sticks. Scotland then got into their stride and scored two more tries through Gary Armstrong and Scott Hastings, with Gavin Hastings and Chalmers adding kicks to win 24–15.

Scotland then faced one of the surprise packages of the

World Cup, Western Samoa, who had shocked Wales and Argentina and had given Australia a real scare before losing 9–3.

'The best we played during the 1991 World Cup was against Western Samoa,' recalled Gavin Hastings. 'They were a good side, they had already beaten Wales, and if you look at all the guys who were playing for them that day, they were a wonderful side. Frank Bunce, Steve Bachop, Pat Lam, Peter Fatialofa – these guys were all playing provincial rugby in New Zealand, so they were playing a far higher standard of rugby week-in and week-out than anyone in the Scotland set-up was. We knew that we had to be at our very best if we were to have any chance and in the end we gave them an absolute doing, 28–6. I think we would have beaten anyone in the world that day.'

This set up a mouth-watering semi-final against England, back at Murrayfield. But after the harum-scarum match of 1990, England had tightened up their game and strangled the life out of Scotland in the spring of 1991. They approached the semi-final in the same manner, utilising their superior forward strength and relying on the boot of Rob Andrew. It may not have been pretty, but it was text-book tournament rugby.

However, with the game still very much in the balance at 6–6 going into the final quarter, Scotland won a penalty in front of the posts. Just a few moments earlier, English flanker Mickey Skinner had felled Gavin Hastings with a huge tackle that required some attention from the physio. Hastings pulled himself to his feet to take the kick – and then pushed it wide.

England had escaped and they began to move back downfield. Several minutes later the ball was fired out to Andrew, who let fly with a booming drop-goal that bisected the posts to give England a 9–6 lead that they didn't relinquish. Scotland had come agonisingly close to appearing in a World Cup final, and now had to satisfy themselves with a third/fourth place play-off match against New Zealand in Cardiff, which they ultimately lost 13–6.

A disconsolate Gavin Hastings at full-time in the 1991 World Cup semi-final.

48

The last four-point try in world rugby

The second Test of Scotland's 1992 summer tour to Australia was notable for several reasons. Not only did David Sole lead Scotland for a 24th time, which set a new record for captaincy of the national team, but he did so for the last time before retirement – a landmark that he celebrated by scoring the last try of the game, which also proved to be the last four-point try in world rugby history.

49

Scotland's first five-point try

Tony Stanger scored Scotland's first five-point try in the 15–3 victory over Ireland at Murrayfield at the beginning of the 1993 Five Nations. Stanger won 52 caps over a long and distinguished career and, as of September 2018, remains the country's joint top try-scorer of all time (with Ian Smith) with 24 tries. He scored arguably the most famous try in Scottish rugby history to win the Grand Slam in 1990 and represented the British & Irish Lions on their victorious tour to South Africa in 1997, before retiring from Test rugby in the aftermath of the 1998 Five Nations.

50

STAT ZONE

Try-scoring record

The record for the most Test tries scored by a Scotland player is held jointly by Ian Smith and Tony Stanger with 24 each:

Ian Smith
3 v Wales at Inverleith, 2 Feb 1924
4 v France at Inverleith, 24 Jan 1925
4 v Wales at Swansea, 7 Feb 1925
2 v England at Twickenham, 20 Mar 1926
2 v France at Murrayfield, 22 Jan 1927
2 v England at Murrayfield, 19 Mar 1927
1 v Ireland at Lansdowne Road, 23 Feb 1929
2 v England at Murrayfield, 16 Mar 1929
2 v England at Murrayfield, 21 Mar 1931
1 v England at Twickenham, 19 Mar 1932
1 v Wales at Swansea, 4 Feb 1933

Tony Stanger
2 v Fiji at Murrayfield, 28 Oct 1989
3 v Romania at Murrayfield, 9 Dec 1989
1 v England at Murrayfield, 17 Mar 1990

1 v New Zealand at Eden Park, 23 Jun 1990
2 v Argentina at Murrayfield, 10 Nov 1990
1 v Ireland at Murrayfield, 16 Mar 1991
1 v Japan at Murrayfield, 5 Oct 1991
1 v Zimbabwe at Murrayfield, 9 Oct 1991
1 v Samoa at Murrayfield, 19 Oct 1991
1 v Ireland at Lansdowne Road, 15 Feb 1992
1 v Ireland at Murrayfield, 16 Jan 1993
1 v South Africa at Murrayfield, 19 Nov 1994
2 v Romania at Murrayfield, 22 Apr 1995
1 v Ivory Coast at Rustenberg, 26 May 1995
1 v Australia at Murrayfield, 9 Nov 1996
1 v Italy at Murrayfield, 14 Dec 1996
1 v Ireland at Murrayfield, 1 Mar 1997
1 v France at Murrayfield, 21 Feb 1998
1 v England at Murrayfield, 22 Mar 1998

Ian Smith and Tony Stanger.

51

FAMOUS FIRSTS

Women's Test rugby

Despite having played their first match as a national side in 1989, global recognition of a Scotland women's rugby team came on Valentine's Day 1993 when Scotland Women took on – and beat – their Irish counterparts in the first official international for both countries. The scorer of Scotland's two tries was pint-size scrum-half Sandra Colamartino, who also captained her country in front of a crowd of more than 1,000 at Raeburn Place.

The head coach for that debut international and over the following five years was Mark Francis, husband of another of the internationalists from that first side, Debbie. Born in Bristol to Scottish parents, she was selected for the fledgling Great Britain women's rugby team. With no official Scotland side, she went on to play for England, out of Leeds, and competed in the first women's Rugby World Cup in 1991. Debbie switched to her 'home' nation two years later and went on to win 35 caps in total – 15 for Scotland, 12 with England and eight in GB colours.

The 1993/94 season began with the successful formation of the Scottish Women's Rugby Union (SWRU) and, after

Holland pulled out of hosting the 1994 (and second) Women's World Cup, Scotland stepped in. The squad was based at Cramond with matches held at various grounds throughout Edinburgh. Scotland's opener against Russia, which they won, also introduced the coaching staff to dynamic Russian captain Rimma Lewis (nee Petlevannaia), who had Scottish residency, was married to a Scot and would be eligible for Scotland two years later. Sure enough she made her debut, against the Netherlands, in 1996 and went on to represent Scotland at three World Cups.

The summer of 1995 saw the debut of the Home Nations Championship between the Welsh, Irish, Scottish and English unions (the French would join two years later), with the first match against Ireland the following January. One of the try-scorers in that away win was wing/full-back and all-round women's rugby stalwart, Sue Brodie. A club player from 1989 to 1998 for Clifton WRFC, Liberton WRFC, Edinburgh WRFC and Edinburgh Academicals WRFC, Brodie was also chairperson of the SWRU, chaired the organising committee for the Women's Rugby World Championship in 1994 and had won her first cap in Scotland's first international in 1993.

The side's first appearance in a European Championship came in 1997 in Nice, and featured the kicking skills of new scrum-half Paula Chalmers. Brother of rugby internationalist Craig, and already capped for Scotland in hockey, Paula went on to be player of the tournament at the European Championship in 2001 and retired after the 2006 World Cup in Canada, having made more appearances in the international jersey than her brother.

1998 saw the Scots win the home international competition with a resounding Grand Slam to boot. Pivotal to the side was Donna Kennedy, the back-row from Biggar, who remains Scotland's most capped female internationalist with 115 caps – and who, for many years, was also the most capped female in the rugby world.

Scotland have appeared in five World Cups, the most recent being 2010 in England – where first to touch down in the tournament was Wick-born solicitor Lucy Millard. The try-machine had notched nine touchdowns as Scotland won the FIRA/AER European Trophy in Sweden in 2009 and was in the Rugby Ecosse team who won the Dubai sevens the following year.

In 2011, ex-international forward Karen 'Jock' Findlay took over head coach duties. The Met Police Chief Inspector (who was in the Scotland team that won the European Championship in France and the Richmond team that won the English Cup final at Twickenham in the same weekend in 2001) introduced a promising young back-row – who was to make history – into the squad during her final season in charge. Jade Konkel, Inverness native and all-round athlete, became Scotland's first full-time professional female player in the summer of 2016 and went on to join French outfit Lille (LMRCV) the following year, paving the way for fellow internationals Chloe Rollie and Lisa Thomson to join the same side and for Sarah Law to become Scotland's fourth professional female player. In July 2018, Scottish Rugby doubled the number of contracted female players, awarding an extension to Konkel's existing contract and adding Sarah Bonar of Loughborough Lightning (11 caps), Megan Kennedy of Stirling County (5 caps), Lisa Martin of LMRCV (41 caps), Helen Nelson of Montpellier (14 caps), Chloe Rollie of LMRCV (22 caps), Lana Skeldon of Watsonians (26 caps), and Lisa Thomson of DMP Sharks (16 caps) to the professional roster.

The wrong side of a Grand Slam showdown

While 1990 will live long in the hearts and minds of Scottish rugby fans, it was not the only time that Scotland played England for the clean sweep. In 1995, Scotland travelled to Twickenham to play England with the Championship title, Calcutta Cup, Triple Crown and Grand Slam once again all on the line.

Just as in 1990, the away team arrived on the back of a stunning victory in Paris. Scotland had secured their first away win over the French in 26 years after Gregor Townsend had performed the 'Toonie Flip' to release Gavin Hastings into space to score under the posts during the dying minutes of the match.

Just as in 1990, it was the visiting team who had been playing electric rugby all Championship, scoring tries from all over the park.

And just as in 1990, it was the home team who emerged victorious to claim the full haul of spoils. Scotland scored twelve points through the boots of Gavin Hastings (two penalties) and Craig Chalmers (two early drop goals), but England emerged victorious thanks to seven penalty goals and a drop-goal by Rob Andrew to win 24–12.

STAT ZONE

World Cup points haul

Gavin Hastings claimed the individual point-scoring record in a single game during Scotland's 89–0 victory over the Ivory Coast at the 1995 World Cup, with 44 points, achieved thanks to two penalties, four tries and nine conversions.

After also defeating Tonga (41–5), Scotland's crunch pool match in the 1995 World Cup was played against France at Loftus Versfeld in Pretoria. A late Émile Ntamack try stole the game for France, who progressed to the quarter-finals as the pool winners thanks to their 22–19 victory. Scotland, meanwhile, had to play the form team of the tournament, New Zealand, at Loftus in the quarter-finals. They were dumped out of the tournament by the All Blacks, 48–30, and the result signalled not only the end of their World Cup journey, but also the end of their full-back's illustrious career. Hastings retired holding an array of Scottish scoring records and, with the captaincy of the 1993 Lions under his belt and his part in the 1990 Grand Slam and the Lions' series victory in Australia in 1989, he will be forever remembered as a true giant of the game.

54

STAT ZONE

Fastest try

Scotland's opening fixture of the 1999 Five Nations (which was the last instalment of the tournament before it expanded to become the Six Nations in 2000 with Italy's inclusion) saw Wales visit Murrayfield. In one of several pre-planned kick-off moves employed by Scotland that season, fly-half Duncan Hodge switched the direction of his kick away from the forwards, who were standing to his right, to target debutant Welsh wing Matthew Robinson. As the ball soared towards the left-hand touchline, there was a moment of confusion between Robinson and Welsh full-back Shane Howarth as both waited for the other to collect the kick; John Leslie, the Scottish centre, plucked the ball from between them and raced away to score. The entire phase was clocked at nine seconds, making it the fastest try ever to be scored in Test history. The try was the catalyst for Scotland's march to the Five Nations title that year. They dispatched Wales 33–20, pushed England all the way at Twickenham before going down 24–21, saw off Ireland 30–13 with a display of superb running rugby at Murrayfield, and then ran riot in Paris to win 36–22.

England went into the final day of the Championship

looking to defeat Wales to secure the Grand Slam, but a superb performance from the men in red culminated in a late try by centre Scott Gibbs that not only denied England the Grand Slam but also handed Scotland the title on points difference.

John Leslie races into the record books as he scored against Wales after just nine seconds.

FAMOUS FIRSTS

The personal clean sweep

The 1999 Five Nations win was notable for many reasons for Scotland, but among the key statistics was Gregor Townsend's remarkable feat of scoring a try in every match. Although Italy wouldn't join the tournament for another year, Scotland played them in a friendly at Murrayfield midway through the 1999 Championship (during one of the fallow weeks when the other four teams were playing); Scotland won 30–12 and Townsend once again scored a try, completing a unique personal Six Nations Grand Slam.

The Scotland captain who helped England win the World Cup

Jim Greenwood was first capped against France in the 1952 Five Nations and went on to win 20 caps for Scotland between 1952 and 1959, when he also toured with the 1955 Lions (playing in all four Tests) and appeared for the Barbarians. His exploits on the field are not, however, where he established his real legacy, but rather through his career as a coach and as a rugby writer. After stints teaching at Glenalmond College, Cheltenham College and Tiffin School in Kingston upon Thames, where, in 1967, he wrote *Improve Your Rugby*, he became a lecturer at Loughborough University and helped establish the university as one of the world's great rugby nurseries. Both Clive Woodward and Andy Robinson studied under him at Loughborough and both hailed him as a rugby genius who greatly influenced their approach to playing and coaching. Woodward declared that no man had done more than Greenwood to transform the modern game with his philosophy of Total Rugby, where every player on the pitch should be highly skilled, athletic and able to influence the game – a hallmark of Woodward's world-dominating England sides of 2000-03. Greenwood's book *Total Rugby* (1978) is considered the bible of rugby coaching all around the world from Auckland to Buenos Aires. '*Total Rugby* is the only rugby coaching book I've ever read,' said Woodward. 'It was way ahead of its time.'

With the exception of the Calcutta Cup match in 2000, it must have been bittersweet at times for Greenwood to watch his former pupil deliver his philosophies so completely, with Woodward's sides regularly dismantling Scotland during his tenure, notching up 26 tries and a total of 218 points over seven matches. His pride at watching those philosophies guide England to the pinnacle of the world rankings and drive them to World Cup success in 2003, however, must have been considerable. And in Scotland we can only ponder what might have been had Greenwood been offered a role – any role – in senior rugby in his homeland.

Greenwood's impact on the game was recognised in 2014 when he was inducted into the World Rugby Hall of Fame.

The doctor will see you now

Dr James Robson has been an intrinsic part of Scottish rugby for more than 25 years. He started working with the national side in 1991 and six years later he shot into public consciousness when the fly-on-the-wall documentary *Living with Lions* was released following the 1997 Lions tour to South Africa, where he appeared as one of the central characters. In total, Robson has overseen more than 200 Scotland games and has toured with the Lions six times (in 1993, 1997, 2001, 2005, 2009 and 2013). A genial and very popular member of every backroom staff he has worked with, he has also proved himself heroic in preventing two fatalities on the field. During the 1997 Lions tour he saved the life of Will Greenwood when the rookie England centre was knocked unconscious in a tackle against the Orange Free State and swallowed his tongue. He was similarly incisive in saving the life of Thom Evans – and also preventing paralysis – when the Scotland wing broke his neck playing against Wales in 2010. He was awarded an MBE in 2017 for his long and continuing service to the game.

The greatest Scottish XV
that never was

Over the years the quality of the Scottish team has been improved markedly with the inclusion of foreign-born players who qualify to wear the thistle thanks to Scottish parents or grandparents, or who have qualified for their adopted country via the residency rule. But there have also been a number of great players who qualified for Scotland but chose to play for other countries. A XV of those unselected players could consist of the following:

15. Mike Gilbert (New Zealand 1935-36), born on the Isle of Bute

14. Matt Banahan (England 2009-11). A bit of the cheat this one, but as he was born in the Channel Islands, Banahan – like Budge Pountney before him – is eligible to play for any of the four Home Unions

13. Mathew Tait (England 2005-10), grandfather from Glasgow

12. Terry Lineen (New Zealand 1957-60), father from Orkney

11. Jason Robinson (England 2001-07), mother from Kirkintilloch

10. Pat Lambie (South Africa 2010-16), grandparents from Troon

9. Dave Loveridge (New Zealand 1978-85), grandparents from Ayrshire

8. Andy Leslie (New Zealand 1974-76), parents both Scottish

7. Cliff Porter (New Zealand, captain of the 1924/25 Invincibles), born and raised in Edinburgh

6. Wayne 'Buck' Shelford (New Zealand 1986-90), grandparents from the Highlands

5. John Currie (England 1956-62), parents both Scottish

4. Ali Williams (New Zealand 2002-12), grandmother from Galashiels

3. Keith Murdoch (New Zealand 1970-72), mother from Edinburgh, father from Springside, Ayrshire

2. Andy Dalton (New Zealand 1977-85), grandfather from the Borders

1. Billy Bush (New Zealand 1974-79), grandfather from Stonehaven

Subs and alternative picks:

Full-back: **Richard Wilson** (New Zealand 1979), **Jock Cuthill** (New Zealand 1913)

Centre: **Ronald Hope Bridie** (Wales 1882)

Fly-half: **Tommaso Allan** (Italy 2013-18), **Neil McGregor** (New Zealand 1924-25), **Doug Bruce** (New Zealand 1976-78), **Eddie Dunn** (New Zealand 1979-81), **Ian Dunn** (New Zealand 1983), **Laurie Haig** (New Zealand 1950-54)

Scrum-half: **Lee Dickson** (England 2012-14), **Jimmy Haig** (New Zealand 1946), **Nigel Melville** (England 1984-88)

Back-row: **Aaron Shingler** (Wales 2012-18)

Second-row: **James Stuart** (Argentina 2007-08), **George Biagi** (Italy 2014-18), **Tom Palmer** (England 2001-12), **John Fleming** (New Zealand 1979-80)

Hooker: **John Black** (New Zealand 1977-80)

Prop: **Jamie Mackintosh** (New Zealand 2008), **Ray Dalton** (New Zealand 1947), **Dale McIntosh** (Wales 1996-97)

Coach: **Clive Woodward** (Woodward's first school was Corstorphine Primary in Edinburgh, so he qualifies on residency)

The most-capped XV

Although several players appeared for Scotland in more than one position, a XV made up of Scotland's most-capped players (totalling, as of July 2018, 1,199 appearances) could read as follows:

15. Chris Paterson (109 caps)
14. Kenny Logan (70 caps)
13. Scott Hastings (65 caps)
12. Gregor Townsend (82 caps)
11. Sean Lamont (105 caps)
10. Dan Parks (67 caps)
9. Mike Blair (85 caps)
8. Simon Taylor (66 caps)
7. John Barclay (68 caps)
6. Jason White (77 caps)
5. Nathan Hines (77 caps)
4. Scott Murray (87 caps)
3. Euan Murray (66 caps)
2. Ross Ford (110 caps)
1. Allan Jacobsen (65 caps)

60

Scotland's highest-scoring win

Scotland ran riot against Japan at McDiarmid Park in Perth in the autumn of 2004, scoring 15 tries, 11 conversions and a lone penalty in a 100–8 victory. Try scorers: Mike Blair, Andy Henderson, Ali Hogg, Sean Lamont, Donnie Macfadyen, Graeme Morrison, Dan Parks, Chris Paterson (3), Jon Petrie, Robbie Russell (2), Hugo Southwell (2). Eleven conversions and penalty: Chris Paterson.

Donnie Macfadyen makes a break against Japan at McDiarmid Park.

STAT ZONE

Scotland's lowest-scoring result

on 18 January 1964 the All Blacks arrived at Murrayfield for the 26th match of a 36-match tour. They had, like pretty much every All Black side before or since, played some scintillating rugby and although they had suffered a surprise loss against Newport in their third game they had quickly recovered to hammer their way past every other side they faced. The crowd that packed into Murrayfield probably expected more of the same. What they got was a remarkable 0–0 stalemate. If it weren't for the fact that the draw remains one of only two occasions when Scotland have avoided defeat against New Zealand in a Test match (the other being the 25–25 draw in 1983), it would be a result that very few rugby fans would ever want to talk about. It also meant that the All Blacks failed to make it a clean sweep in their Test matches on the tour, as they had already dispatched Ireland, Wales and England before the match at Murrayfield, and would go on to defeat France three weeks later. So as dull as the game might have been, it remains (something of) a feather in Scotland's cap.

62

STAT ZONE

Scotland's highest-scoring victory over a southern hemisphere team

In the summer of 2017, Scotland performed superbly to defeat Australia 24–19 in Sydney with a display of power, incisive running lines, deft handling and fearsome defence. That autumn, the Wallabies travelled to Murrayfield looking for revenge. Scotland had pushed New Zealand all the way a week earlier before going down 22–17. Stuart Hogg, who had been Scotland's most dangerous player against the All Blacks and had almost created a winning score in the dying seconds, was all set to cause mayhem against Australia; but he was ruled out just ten minutes before kick-off when he injured himself during the warm-up. In a last-minute reshuffle, Sean Maitland moved to full-back and Byron McGuigan came on to the wing to make his first start for Scotland. Despite the late change, Scotland showed their burgeoning class to hit their straps from the off, with McGuigan scoring an early try. The Aussies bounced back with two tries of their own, scored by Tevita Kuridrani to lead 12–10 as half-time approached.

But the game changed just moments before the break when Sekope Kepu flew into a ruck and used his shoulder to clear out Hamish Watson. Television replays showed that Kepu had made direct contact with Watson's head and referee Pascal Gaüzère had no choice but to show the Wallaby tight-head a red card. Scotland, buoyed by their one-man advantage, put their foot on the accelerator and never looked back. From the Kepu penalty they kicked to the corner, set up a maul and Ali Price darted over to take a 17–12 lead into half-time. The break did nothing to stall their momentum and they went on to score a further six tries in the second half through Maitland, Jonny Gray, Huw Jones, a second for McGuigan, John Barclay and Stuart McInally to record a final scoreline of 53–24 and end the year on an unprecedented high.

Captain John Barclay roars with delight as he scores one of Scotland's eight tries against the Wallabies.

63

STAT ZONE

Scotland's highest winning margin against a Six Nations opponent

Probably unsurprisingly (sorry, Azzurri fans), this was achieved against Italy. The highest scoring margin that Scotland have ever recorded against the Italians came in August 2015 as part of that year's World Cup preparations, when the Scots won 48–7 at Murrayfield; but in the Six Nations, the record was set in 2017 with a 29–0 win, also at Murrayfield. The try scorers that day were Finn Russell, Matt Scott, Tim Visser and Tommy Seymour, with Russell converting three of these and Stuart Hogg adding a long-range penalty.

Tommy Seymour flies in to score Scotland's bonus-point try against Italy during the 2017 Six Nations match at Murrayfield.

64

Scotland's largest losing margin

In November 1997, the reigning world champions, South Africa, embarked on a tour of the northern hemisphere under a new coach in Nick Mallett and with a steely determination to right the wrongs of their Test series loss to the Lions four months earlier. Having dispatched Italy (62–31), France twice (36–32 and 52–10) and England (29–11) they came to Murrayfield for their final fixture of the year – and decimated the hosts 68–10 with a comprehensive display of power, speed and skill. It was their fifth win in a row (having also defeated the Lions in the final game of the three-match series) and they wouldn't lose again for another whole year as they put together a 17-match winning streak. That we were clearly in the presence of greatness that day didn't help salve the feeling of utter wretchedness among the home fans. It was a tough old watch.

As a personal segue down memory lane, it was also the first time I'd painted my face to go and see a game. In light of the result, it was also the last.

65

Points machine

Not only is Chris Paterson one of a very select band of centurions (just three players have reached this landmark of caps to date), but he is also Scotland's record points scorer, with 809 points notched up over a 12-year (1999-2011) and 109-Test career. This haul includes three drop-goals, 22 tries, 90 conversions and 170 penalties. He also holds the Scottish record for the most points scored in a single Five or Six Nations Championship with 65, achieved in 2007 thanks to one try, six conversions and 16 penalties.

Later that year he began a new Test rugby kicking record, slotting 36 successive shots at goal between August 2007 and June 2008. I can remember going to Murrayfield in the late spring of 1999 to watch him play for Gala in the Scottish Cup final and thinking, 'This skinny guy at full-back is pretty good.' I know, my forensically detailed level of analysis has always been impressive. After scoring the only try of the game and a drop-goal to win the cup – to add to the winner's medal he picked at the Melrose Sevens a few weeks earlier – he is one of the last players to have gone straight from amateur club rugby to the Scotland set-up when he was selected for that summer's tour to South Africa. And all this while Gala were still playing in the second division. He turned pro with Glasgow for the 1999/2000 season (before switching to Edinburgh after two games), was selected for the 1999 World Cup squad and won his first cap against Spain. *Boy's Own* stuff. I knew he'd go far . . .

He would retire after Scotland's final game in the 2011 World Cup – a pool defeat to England that meant Scotland failed to qualify for the knock-out rounds for the first time in their World Cup history. It was an underwhelming end to a magnificent career, but it does not tarnish the regard that Paterson will be held in by the Scottish rugby community.

Forwards scoring like backs

In my playing days, I was a prop. And, like many props, I had very little interest in rucking and mauling and a lot of interest in swanning around in the backs, thinking I was Carlos Spencer. Consequently, I appreciate it when the big men up front display the kind of skill and élan that is usually the preserve of only the finest backs. The following moments are classic examples of my heroes in action:

Dropping goals: Charles Cathcart (against England in 1872), John Boswell (against Ireland in 1890 and England in 1893), Saxon McEwan (against Ireland in 1891), and Peter Kininmonth (against Wales in 1951) have all scored drop-goals for Scotland while also taking care of things up front as part of the pack. What a bunch of legends. Kininmonth's was particularly famous as it it did set Scotland on the path to a 19-0 win against Wales at Murrayfield – but also became a touch infamous, as that was the last match that Scotland won for four years and the moment became something of an albatross for the team over that dreadful period.

Place kicking: I've always loved a regular goal-kicking forward. In recent times the most famous of these has been the great

John Eales from Australia, but his predecessor in the role was Peter 'PC' Brown, Scotland's former second-row/number eight. He had a bizarre kicking ritual that saw him dig a divot in the ground with his heel, quickly place the ball then turn his back on the ball as he vaguely paced out a run up. He'd then turn, wipe his nose, wipe his shorts (don't think too much about it), do a little shuffle and then run-up and melt the ball with a schoolboy-esque toe-poke. And do you know what? It was bloody effective. His most famous kick was probably from the Calcutta Cup match at Twickenham in 1971 when he lined up a conversion to win the game. His late, and much-missed, brother Gordon can take up the story from here: 'It was halfway out, to the left of the posts. I remember standing there just thinking: "Come on, Peter! I've seen you kick that kind of goal hundreds of time. On the beach at Troon. At Marr College. At West. At Murrayfield. Just do it once more! Never mind the usual act of turning your back and walking away from the ball and blowing your nose all over the place.

Just kick the goal. Please! Oh, no. He's turned his back on it. He's blowing his nose. Doesn't he know time's nearly up? He's blowing his nose again! God, he's actually enjoying it! *Bang.* It's over. I love him!" I sprinted towards him to kiss him as I have never kissed him before, but he just pushed me away, screaming: "We've still got a few more minutes to get through!"

'But we did get through it and then I gave him his kiss! The pitch was swarming with Scottish fans. A marvellous mayhem – I loved it.'

Incredible scenes.

Creating tries with the boot: I've only ever seen Peter Brown's conversion and Kininmonth's drop-goal on video, but one of my favourite tries ever scored was created by one of my favourite ever players right before my eyes. The 2001 Six Nations encounter against Wales at Murrayfield is not regarded as a classic . . . but Tom Smith's performance was exactly that. Not only did he do all the basics of a prop forward to a world-class standard, he also scored a try from 22 metres out that helped us draw the game. But the moment I remember him most clearly for was his creation of a try for Chris Paterson when he got the ball on the move inside the Welsh 22, tight to the touchline, and threaded an immaculate grubber kick into the corner for Paterson to pounce and score. What. A. Player.

The naughty step

There have only ever been three red cards in Scottish Test history. The first was given to Nathan Hines against the USA in San Francisco on the 2002 summer tour; the second was shown to Scott Murray against Wales at the Millennium Stadium in 2002; and the third was for Stuart Hogg against Wales at the Millennium Stadium in 2014. While Scotland held on to comfortably defeat the USA 65–23 in 2002, the other cards proved to be game-changing and Scotland lost both matches – the 2002 match 27–22, the 2014 match a hard-to-watch 51–3.

To go with the notoriety of being the first Scotland player to be red-carded, Hines is also the most yellow-carded player in Scottish Test history, with five.

Yellow cards are, of course, a more regular feature in the modern game, but there have been eight matches to date where Scotland have been hit with two yellow cards in the same game and they have often proved to be extremely costly:

England at Twickenham, 2003 (lost 40–9)
Wales at the Millennium Stadium, 2010 (lost 31–24)
Wales at the Millennium Stadium, 2012 (lost 27–13)
Italy at the Stadio Olimpico, 2012 (lost 13–6)
Argentina at Murrayfield, 2014 (won 41–31)
Italy at Murrayfield, 2015 (lost 22–19)
Italy at Stadio Olimpico, 2016 (won 36–20)
Ireland at the Aviva Stadium, 2016 (lost 35–25)

69

Shortest career

After the introduction of replacements in 1969, 17 players have won just a single cap off the bench (which is one more cap than most of us have won, so I'm taking nothing away from them):

Bill Macdonald v Ireland, 1969
Steve Turk v England, 1971
Hamish Bryce v Ireland, 1973
Jimmy Gossman v England, 1980
Ian Corcoran v Australia, 1992
Paul Jones v Wales, 1992
Scott Nichol v Argentina, 1994
John Manson v England, 1995
Cameron Glasgow v France, 1997
Andrew Hall v USA, 2002
Andrew Dall v Wales, 2003
Andrew Wilson v Romania, 2005
Jack Cuthbert v Ireland, 2011
Tom Brown v Australia, 2012
Steven Lawrie v South Africa, 2013
Tyrone Holmes v South Africa, 2014
Phil Burleigh v Australia, 2017

GOLDEN OLDIES

Scotland's oldest debutant

Andrew Ker, aged 33 years and 127 days, made his Scotland debut against Wales at the Cardiff Arms Park in 1988. The fly-half won two caps (starting both games), the second coming later that season against England at Murrayfield. Both matches were lost, 25–20 and 9–6 respectively.

GOLDEN OLDIES

Scotland's oldest try scorer

When Scotland captain Jim Aitken crossed to score against Wales at Cardiff Arms Park in 1984, he not only helped his side secure the first win of their Grand Slam campaign, but he set the record as Scotland's oldest try-scorer at 36 years and 60 days – a record he still holds to this day.

GOLDEN OLDIES

Scotland's oldest player

When Ian 'Mighty Mouse' McLauchlan ran out for his final Test appearance, against New Zealand at Murrayfield in 1979, he brought down the curtain on a magnificent career that had seen him captain Scotland for (what was then) a record 19 Tests, as well as marking his place in history as an intrinsic part of the legendary winning Lions tours of 1971 and 1974. He was not able to help his side secure a first victory over the All Blacks in that final game, but he did mark the occasion in another way – by setting the record as the oldest player to represent Scotland at 37 years and 210 days.

73

Longevity awards

Full-back William 'Copey' Murdoch holds the record for the longest career in Scottish Test history, having made his debut against England at Murrayfield in 1935, and then playing his final game 13 years and 4 days later, rather neatly, also against England at Murrayfield in 1948. However, Murdoch's career consisted of only nine Tests (because of the interrupted years of the Second World War).

Two other players are hot on his heels for longevity while also playing considerably more matches for Scotland: Scott Lawson won 47 caps over a span of 12 years and 243 days between 2005 and 2018, and Ross Ford has won a staggering 110 caps over 12 years and 230 days between 2004 and 2017.

Alan Tait, Jim Renwick and Sean Lamont also enjoyed careers that spanned over 12 years and more than 50 caps (and in Lamont's case, 105) between their debuts and their final Test appearances.

So near and yet . . .
Players who only made it as far the bench

Rob Cunningham had the agonising distinction of sitting behind Colin Deans for 51 consecutive Tests . . . and never got capped.

Simon Cross sat on the bench just once for Scotland but got slightly closer to winning a cap than Cunningham did – excruciatingly so. Towards the end of the 2004 Six Nations match against Wales, he was told to remove his tracksuit and he stood pitch-side waiting for the next stoppage in play so that he could run on to the field. However, that passage of play went on for several minutes and by the time it finished, the clock had run into overtime and referee Donal Courtney signalled the end of the game. It still makes me sad to think of how Cross must have felt at the time and how he must look back on that moment of so nearly fulfilling a dream to play Test rugby.

So near and yet ...
Part II

The following players appeared in non-Test matches for Scotland but didn't ever win a full cap:

J Anderson – 1 Victory International, 1946
W Anderson v Spain, 1998
D Ashton v Japan, 1976
AL Barcroft – 2 Service Internationals, 1942-45
WG Biggart – 1 Service International, 1942-45
JM Blair – 3 Service Internationals, 1942-45
J Brannigan v Barbarians, 2002
AWB Buchanan – 2 Service Internationals, 1942-45
D Butcher v Zimbabwe, 1988
J Carswell v Japan, 1976
R Cowe – 3 Service Internationals, 1942-45
S Cranston v Barbarians, 2003
MR Dewar – 2 Service Internationals, 1942-45
A Donaldson v Fiji, 1993
ECK Douglas – 4 Service Internationals, 1942-45
S Ferguson v Fiji 1993, v Tonga 1993 and v Western Samoa, 1993
E Grant – 4 Service Internationals, 1942-45
N Grecian v Fiji, 1993 and v Western Samoa, 1993
SGA Harper – 1 Service International, 1942-45

JR Henderson – 2 Service Internationals, 1942-45

EC Hunter – 2 Service Internationals, 1942-45

G Isaac v Fiji, 1993, v Tonga 1993 and v Western Samoa, 1993

MD Kennedy – 1 Service International, 1942-45

S Johnston v Spain, 1986

J Kirk – 4 Victory Internationals, 1946

R Kirkpatrick v Canada, 1991

B Laidlaw v Argentina, 1969

C Mair v Japan, 1976

J Maltman – 4 Service Internationals, 1942-45

S McAslan v Zimbabwe, 1988

C McClay – 1 Service International, 1942-45

JR McClure – 4 Service Internationals, 1942-45 and 1 Victory International, 1946

RM McKenzie – 2 Service Internationals, 1942-45. [He was, however, capped by New Zealand, winning 9 caps and playing in a further 26 matches for the All Blacks between 1934 and 1938]

R Mclean v Zimbabwe, 1988 and v Japan, 1989

JB McNeil – 2 Service Internationals, 1942-45

EA Melling – 1 Service International, 1942-45

R Moffat v Japan, 1977

M Moncrieff v USA 1991, v Barbarians, 1991, v Tonga 1993 and v Western Samoa 1993

G Morton v Barbarians, 2003

J Murchie v Argentina, 1969

AE Murray – 1 Service International, 1942-45

JB Nicholls – 2 Service Internationals, 1942-45

A Orr v Argentina, 1969

H Parker v Zimbabwe, 1988

K Rafferty v Zimbabwe, 1988

NW Ramsay – 3 Service Internationals, 1942-45

C Redpath v Tonga, 1993

B Renwick v Barbarians, 1991

DA Roberts – 1 Service International, 1942-45

R Scott v Fiji, 1993 and v Western Samoa, 1993

JAD Thom – 1 Service International, 1942-45

HG Uren – 1 Service International, 1942-45

G Waite v Spain, 1986

C Wilhelm – 1 Service International, 1942-45

G Wilson v Japan, 1989

KHS Wilson – 1 Victory International, 1946

76

Super sub

Although he is Scotland's most capped scrum-half (with 85 caps), Mike Blair also has the distinction of holding the record for the most appearances as a sub (20).

Mike Blair in action against Ireland in 2011.

Oh captain, my captain

The following players have had the honour of captaining Scotland in a Test match:

Name	First match as captain
FJ Moncreiff	27 Mar 1871
WD Brown	23 Feb 1874
RW Irvine	6 Mar 1876
JHS Graham	19 Feb 1881
R Ainslie	18 Feb 1882
DY Cassels	4 Mar 1882
WE Maclagan	12 Jan 1884
JB Brown	9 Jan 1886
C Reid	19 Feb 1887
ARD Wauchope	10 Mar 1888
DS Morton	2 Feb 1889
MC McEwan	22 Feb 1890
CE Orr	6 Feb 1892
RG MacMillan	4 Feb 1893
JD Boswell	18 Feb 1893
WR Gibson	26 Jan 1895
GT Neilson	25 Jan 1896
AR Smith	19 Feb 1898
WP Donaldson	18 Feb 1899
MC Morrison	4 Mar 1899

Name	First match as captain
TM Scott	24 Feb 1900
JRC Greenlees	21 Mar 1903
WP Scott	4 Feb 1905
AB Timms	18 Mar 1905
DR Bedell-Sivright	18 Nov 1905
L West	3 Feb 1906
LL Greig	17 Nov 1906
P Munro	23 Feb 1907
IC Geddes	21 Mar 1908
JMB Scott	6 Feb 1909
G Cunningham	20 Mar 1909
GM Frew	5 Feb 1910
JC MacCallum	18 Mar 1911
FH Turner	23 Nov 1912
DM Bain	7 Feb 1914
E Milroy	28 Feb 1914
AW Angus	1 Jan 1920
CM Usher	7 Feb 1920
J Hume	22 Jan 1921
AL Gracie	20 Jan 1923
JCR Buchanan	1 Jan 1924
GPS Macpherson	24 Jan 1925
D Drysdale	28 Feb 1925
JM Bannerman	4 Feb 1928
WN Roughead	24 Jan 1931
WM Simmers	16 Jan 1932
IS Smith	4 Feb 1933
H Lind	3 Feb 1934
MS Stewart	24 Feb 1934
KC Fyfe	2 Feb 1935
RW Shaw	23 Feb 1935
RCS Dick	1 Feb 1936
JA Beattie	21 Mar 1936
WR Logan	6 Feb 1937

Name	First match as captain
KI Geddes	1 Jan 1947
WH Munro	22 Feb 1947
CR Bruce	15 Mar 1947
JRS Innes	22 Nov 1947
DH Keller	15 Jan 1949
WID Elliot	14 Jan 1950
PW Kininmonth	18 Mar 1950
A Cameron	24 Nov 1951
AF Dorward	15 Mar 1952
JNG Davidson	9 Jan 1954
JT Greenwood	8 Jan 1955
AR Smith	23 Feb 1957
GH Waddell	21 Mar 1959
KJF Scotland	12 Jan 1963
JB Neill	4 Jan 1964
MJ Campbell-Lamerton	6 Feb 1965
S Wilson	20 Mar 1965
IHP Laughland	26 Feb 1966
JP Fisher	17 Dec 1966
JW Telfer	16 Mar 1968
FAL Laidlaw	21 Mar 1970
PC Brown	16 Jan 1971
I McLauchlan	3 Feb 1973
IR McGeechan	15 Jan 1977
DW Morgan	21 Jan 1978
MA Biggar	2 Feb 1980
AR Irvine	15 Mar 1980
RJ Laidlaw	15 Jan 1983
J Aitken	5 Mar 1983
DG Leslie	16 Feb 1985
CT Deans	18 Jan 1986
GJ Callander	16 Jan 1988
F Calder	21 Jan 1989
DMB Sole	28 Oct 1989

Name	First match as captain
PW Dods	9 Oct 1991
AG Hastings	16 Jan 1993
AI Reed	4 Jun 1994
RI Wainwright	18 Nov 1995
GPJ Townsend	9 Nov 1996
AD Nicol	22 Nov 1997
G Armstrong	7 Feb 1998
BW Redpath	21 Nov 1998
EW Peters	6 Mar 1999
JA Leslie	5 Feb 2000
AC Pountney	4 Nov 2000
TJ Smith	10 Nov 2001
SB Grimes	15 Jun 2002
S Murray	23 Aug 2003
GC Bulloch	6 Sep 2003
CD Paterson	14 Feb 2004
JM Petrie	5 Jun 2005
JPR White	12 Nov 2005
MRL Blair	23 Feb 2008
CP Cusiter	14 Nov 2009
AD Kellock	12 Jun 2010
RGM Lawson	20 Nov 2010
RW Ford	4 Feb 2012
KDR Brown	11 Nov 2012
GD Laidlaw	15 Jun 2013
GS Gilchrist	20 Jun 2014
HB Pyrgos	15 Aug 2015
AK Strokosch	22 Aug 2015
JA Barclay	25 Feb 2017
SW Hogg	16 Jun 2018
S McInally	23 Jun 2018

78

Oh captain . . . still my captain

As of July 2018, the top ten longest-serving captains (by number of Tests in charge) are:

	Name	Number of matches
1st:	GD Laidlaw	31
2nd:	DMB Sole	25
3rd:	BW Redpath	21
4th:	AG Hastings	20
5th equal:	I McLauchlan	19
5th equal:	JPR White	19
6th:	RI Wainwright	16
7th equal:	AR Irvine	15
7th equal:	MC Morrison	15
7th equal:	AR Smith	15
8th equal:	G Armstrong	14
8th equal:	MRL Blair	14
8th equal:	KDR Brown	14
8th equal:	JA Barclay	14
9th equal:	CT Deans	13
9th equal:	CD Paterson	13
10th:	GPS Macpherson	12

Scottish centurions

Three players have, to date, won more than 100 caps. They are:

Ross Ford, 110 caps
Chris Paterson, 109 caps
Sean Lamont, 105 caps

100th cap to forget

Chris Paterson became Scotland's first rugby centurion when he appeared at full-back against Wales in 2010. It was a game that will live long in the memory – although, unfortunately, not for Paterson's landmark achievement. And it all started so well, too.

After just 12 minutes, John Barclay powered his way between James Hook and Gareth Cooper to score by the posts. Dan Parks then slid an inch-perfect grubber behind the Welsh defence for Max Evans to score in the corner and Scotland were 15–3 up inside the first quarter. Just after half-time, and with Parks kicking like a dream, Scotland were 21–9 up. With four minutes to go, Scotland were 24–14 to the good. But listing scores like this doesn't do any justice to the story of the match – or the horrific luck suffered by Scotland. First, Paterson went down injured after just 15 minutes, a lacerated kidney eventually forcing him off, even though he tried to play through the pain. An ankle injury to Rory Lamont ended both his game and his season. And then Thom Evans, most shockingly, suffered a near-fatal spinal injury that ultimately led to his retirement from the game; it was thanks only to the work of Dr James Robson on the field, and the staff at both the Millennium Stadium and Cardiff University Hospital that Evans is both alive and able to walk.

Because of the raft of injuries, Scotland ended up employing four different full-backs during the game and finished the match with just four backs on the field – and 13 men, with replacements Scott Lawson and Phil Godman both in the sin-bin.

There were just 12 seconds of normal time remaining when a stray Godman boot tripped Lee Byrne after the Welsh full-back chipped ahead. Godman was sent to the side lines and Stephen Jones kicked the penalty to tie the scores. Scotland restarted, with replacement scrum-half Mike Blair – who played the whole of the second half on the wing – handed kicking duties. Wales gathered, kicked to the corner, regained possession and kept recycling. Scotland simply ran out of numbers and eventually wing Shane Williams went in under the posts to snatch one of the most dramatic wins in Championship history – and perhaps the most painful one for Scotland.

STAT ZONE

Fifty cap club

The following players have won 50 or more caps for Scotland (not including Lions caps; centurions are listed in fact number 79):

Scott Murray, 87 caps
Mike Blair, 85 caps
Gregor Townsend, 82 caps
Nathan Hines, 77 caps
Jason White, 77 caps
Gordon Bulloch, 75 caps
Stuart Grimes, 71 caps
John Barclay, 71 caps
Chris Cusiter, 70 caps
Kenny Logan, 70 caps
Dan Parks, 67 caps
Euan Murray, 66 caps
Simon Taylor, 66 caps
Scott Hastings, 65 caps
Allan Jacobsen, 65 caps
Kelly Brown, 64 caps
Richie Gray, 64 caps
Greig Laidlaw, 63 caps
Jim Hamilton, 63 caps

Stuart Hogg, 62 caps
Gavin Hastings, 61 caps
Tom Smith, 61 caps
Doddie Weir, 61 caps
Craig Chalmers, 60 caps
Bryan Redpath, 60 caps
Hugo Southwell, 59 caps
Alasdair Dickinson, 58 caps
Alastair Kellock, 56 caps
Andy Henderson, 53 caps
Paul Burnell, 52 caps
Colin Deans, 52 caps
Jim Renwick, 52 caps
Tony Stanger, 52 caps
Gary Armstrong, 51 caps
Andy Irvine, 51 caps
Sandy Carmichael, 50 caps
Gavin Kerr, 50 caps

STAT ZONE

Most Five or Six Nations Championship appearances

Ross Ford, 55
Chris Paterson, 53
Sean Lamont, 45
Scott Murray, 43
Gregor Townsend, 43

STAT ZONE

Scotland in the Six Nations

There have been no Championship titles, Grand Slams or Triple Crowns to date for Scotland in the Six Nations, but their other achievements are listed below (up to and including the 2018 Six Nations):

Calcutta Cups: **4** (2000, 2006, 2008, 2018)
Centenary Quaichs: **4** (2001, 2010, 2013, 2017)
Wooden Spoon 'winners': **4** 2004, 2007, 2012, 2015
Total games played: **95**
Won: **27** (win rate 25.7%)
Tries: **127**
Conversions: **96**
Penalties: **243**
Drop-goals: **15**

84

Scotland at the World Cup

Gavin Hastings holds all the major records for a Scotland player at the World Cup, having played in 13 games across three tournaments (1987, 1991 and 1995), and scored 227 points (placing him second on the all-time points list behind Jonny Wilkinson). Other players to appear in three World Cups include:

Chris Paterson (1999, 2003 and 2007)
Mike Blair (2003, 2007 and 2011)
Paul Burnell (1991, 1995 and 1999)
Ross Ford (2007, 2011 and 2015)
Scott Hastings (1987, 1991 and 1995)
Nathan Hines (2003, 2007 and 2011)
Sean Lamont (2007, 2011 and 2015)
Kenny Logan (1995, 1999 and 2003)
Scott Murray (1999, 2003 and 2007)
Bryan Redpath (1995, 1999 and 2003)
Doddie Weir (1991, 1995 and 1999)

World Cup record

Scotland have only once failed to emerge from the pool stages at the World Cup (in 2011) and have subsequently been knocked out at the quarter-final stage on six occasions, and the semi-final stage on one occasion (giving them the opportunity, in 1991, to play New Zealand for third place, although they lost 13–6).

1987 – quarter-final exit, losing 30–3 to New Zealand at Lancaster Park.

1991 – semi-final exit, losing 9–6 to England at Murrayfield.

1995 – quarter-final exit, losing 48–30 to New Zealand at Loftus Versfeld.

1999 – quarter-final exit, losing 30–18 to New Zealand at Murrayfield.

2003 – quarter-final exit, losing 33–16 to Australia at Suncorp Stadium.

2007 – quarter-final exit, losing 19–13 to Argentina at the Stade de France.

2011 – pool stage exit, losing 13–12 to Argentina at the Westpac Stadium and 16–12 to England at Eden Park.

2015 – quarter-final exit, losing 35–34 to Australia at Twickenham.

Mark Bennett intercepts a pass from prop James Slipper to scorch away to score what, at this stage, looked like the match-winning try against Australia at the 2015 World Cup. Scotland would go on to lose to a late – and controversial – Bernard Foley penalty.

86

The head honcho

Since Bill Dickinson was appointed as Scotland's first coach (or rather, at the time, 'the adviser to the captain') in 1971, there have been a total of 12 Scotland head coaches, with both Jim Telfer and Ian McGeechan enjoying two stints in the role. They are as follows:

Name	Tenure	Matches	Won	Drew	Lost	Win %
Bill Dickinson	1971–77	27	14	0	13	52
Nairn McEwan	1977–80	14	1	2	11	7
Jim Telfer	1980–84	27	13	2	12	52
Colin Telfer	1984–85	6	0	0	6	0
Derrick Grant	1985–88	18	9	1	8	50
Ian McGeechan	1988–93	33	19	1	13	58
Jim Telfer	1994–99	53	21	2	30	40
Ian McGeechan	2000–03	43	18	1	24	42
Matt Williams	2003–05	17	3	0	14	18
Frank Hadden	2005–09	41	16	0	25	39
Andy Robinson	2009–12	35	15	1	19	43
Scott Johnson	2012–14	16	5	0	11	31
Vern Cotter	2014–17	36	19	0	17	53
Gregor Townsend	2017–18	14	9	0	5	64

STAT ZONE

Scotland's Five Nations record

The Five Nations was contested between 1910 and 1999 (with a break between 1932 and 1939 when the French were temporarily expelled on the suspicion of professionalism in their domestic game). Scotland's key records for the tournament are:

Grand Slams: **3** (1925, 1984, 1990)

Championship wins (non-Grand Slam): **2** (1929, 1999)

Championship wins (shared title): **6** (1920, shared with England and Wales; 1926, shared with Ireland; 1927, shared with Ireland; 1964, shared with Wales; 1973, shared between all five teams; 1986, shared with France)

Triple Crowns: **3** (1925, 1984, 1990)

88

Record points on debut

Gordon Ross made his debut at fly-half for Scotland against Tonga in 2001 and broke the record points haul for an individual in a single match with 23, scoring five penalties and four conversions in a 43–20 victory. He would go on to win 25 caps in a five-year Test career.

Gordon Ross attempts to escape the clutches of the Tongan defence during his remarkable debut in 2001.

Nefarious tricks and tactics

Now, as much as we like to think of rugby as a game of values, played by ladies and gentlemen of unquestionable moral fibre, there have, on occasion, been times when Scottish rugby has strayed from the straight and narrow and into the murky world of gamesmanship, rule-bending and creative interpretation. Without wishing to create an exhaustive list of litanies, here are some less-than-glorious examples of when we have taken advantage of febrile atmospheres and loopholes in the rules:

Dubious tries, part one: In 1990, Tony Stanger scored the most famous try in Scottish rugby history. Or did he? TV angles are limited – and therefore inconclusive – but there is an air of doubt over whether Stanger did in fact ground the ball with his outstretched arm. Gavin Hastings has aired his doubts ('I was bundled into touch after putting in the kick ahead, so I didn't ever see Tony touch it down – and of course some people still argue that he didn't touch it down at all. You wonder in these days of television replays whether it would have been given, but it would have taken a brave man to disallow that score') but Stanger remains resolute. 'It was definitely a try,' he said. 'I remember being given a try against Australia in 1996 when I was tackled over the touchline and didn't get the ball down' – perhaps this try should be added to the list of misdemeanours in this section – 'but the referee gave the score. I was very aware at the time that it shouldn't have been a score, so you instinctively know when a try should be given and when it shouldn't – and I instinctively knew at the time that it was definitely a try.'

Let's just be thankful that there wasn't a TMO back then (or in 1996) . . .

Dubious tries, part two: The roar that reverberated around Murrayfield when Stanger scored in 1990 no doubt convinced referee David Bishop of its legitimacy. It is human nature to be swayed by such matters. It is arguable that referee Nigel Williams was similarly convinced in 2002 when Scotland defeated South Africa for the first time in 33 years. First Nikki Walker claimed to have laid a finger on a loose ball (which was deliberated over for an age by the TMO before it was given), and then Budge Pountney claimed a try while lying at the bottom of a heap of bodies. The shrill yells of delight from the Scottish players around Pountney definitely played a part in Williams awarding a try that he couldn't see at the time and which TV replays were unable to verify, and around which there was a considerable amount of doubt. But the enthusiastic cries did the trick and Williams blew his whistle for the five points as Scotland pushed on for a famous 21–6 victory.

No narrow win: Scotland played Australia four times in 2004 – twice on tour in the summer and twice in the autumn. Scotland lost both the tour games, going down 35–15 in Melbourne and then 34–13 in Sydney; by the time the third game came around at Murrayfield, head coach Matt Williams was getting desperate. So desperate in fact that, in an attempt to stifle the Wallabies' dangerous outside backs, he had the touchlines at Murrayfield painted over and new ones put in at the legal minimum width, making the pitch significantly narrower than normal. 'It still makes me cringe to think about it,' recalls flanker Donnie Macfadyen, who played in all four encounters. 'And it made no difference in the end because they still hammered us.' That they did, winning 31–14 before also recording a 31–17 victory in Glasgow to secure a clean sweep over Scotland that year (and something of a consistent trend on the scoreboard).

Who's your granny? Ever since the dawn of Test rugby, there have been a huge number of players who have had some fairly shaky connections to the country they played Test rugby for – and, indeed, many players have represented more than one country during their careers.

While this practice was often little commented on, the whole issue around eligibility came to a crescendo in 2000 with the so-called 'Grannygate' scandal.

At the centre of the storm were David Hilton of Scotland, and Shane Howarth and Brett Sinkinson of Wales, who it was discovered had no actual qualifications to play for these countries. Howarth had already won four caps for the All Blacks in 1994 before switching his allegiance to Wales, based on his belief that his mother's father was from Cardiff.

Sinkinson, meanwhile, believed that his grandfather had been born in Carmarthen, but it was later discovered that all four of his grandparents, like Howarth's, were born in New Zealand.

Hilton was born in Bristol and believed that he qualified

for Scotland through his grandfather, who the family believed had been born in Edinburgh.

'There was never any doubt in my mind at the time that I was Scottish qualified, none at all,' he recalled. 'I was so confident that I offered to produce my grandfather's birth certificate. I phoned up my dad and he said he didn't have a copy of the birth certificate but the Edinburgh registrar could easily get it. So I got in touch with them and they said they needed my great grandfather's name, which was a bit odd. They found his name but not my great grandmother because she was married three times and it was a bit of a struggle to discover which name she was under. Then eventually they told me there was no record of a Walter Hilton being born in Edinburgh. I asked, "What about the rest of Scotland?" and she said, "That does cover the whole of Scotland".

'Even then I was hoping and hoping. Then my dad eventually got hold of the death certificate and there it was, Walter Hilton had been born in Bristol. We'd always thought he was born in Edinburgh but he was registered in Bristol and his birth date and date of registration were 16 weeks apart and a lot could have happened in that time. The reason I got banned was because we couldn't prove that he was born in Scotland but in the same breath no one could prove that he wasn't.'

Several other high-profile players were also caught up in the scandal, including Wales flanker Colin Charvis, who had been first capped for Wales in 1996. It was later discovered that Charvis had been ineligible at the time, but by the time the scandal broke, he had completed the required three-year residency period and no further action was taken against him.

While Howarth never played for Wales again, both Hilton

and Sinkinson endured the public humiliation of the scandal, saw out their residency periods and came back to play for their adopted countries again.

'I kept at it and worked away until I could qualify by residency – and just hoped that my time would come again,' said Hilton. 'It took to 2002 until I was cleared to play for Scotland again and I won my 42nd cap against South Africa at Murrayfield. I wasn't at my best but it was great that Scotland didn't turn their back on me and I was very determined to prove I should be there. I played 15 minutes off the bench and the crowd reaction was brilliant. It was one of my favourite games for Scotland and the pride I had at helping us beat South Africa 21–6 for the first time in 33 years was unbelievable. I didn't win any more caps after that but it was all worth it.'

It was undoubtedly a proud moment for Hilton, but the whole period had been a dark one for the game – and it is an issue that has reared its head on occasion ever since – most recently when both Spain and Russia were ejected from playing in the 2019 Rugby World Cup because they had fielded ineligible players during the qualification games. With World Rugby's complicated eligibility laws in place and without a central global register of players, it looks set to be an issue that may well come to the fore again in years to come.

Bleeding for the Thistle

(and the Rose ... and the Springbok ... and the Silver Fern ... and the Wallaby)

The following players have won caps for Scotland as well as for other countries:

James Marsh – 2 caps for Scotland (1889) and 1 cap for England (1892)

Bill McEwan – 16 caps for Scotland (1894-1900) and 2 caps for South Africa (1903)

Alex Frew – 3 caps for Scotland (1901) and 1 cap for South Africa (1903)

Colin Gilray – 1 cap for New Zealand (1905) and 4 caps for Scotland (1908-12)

Don Macpherson – 1 cap for New Zealand (1905) and 2 caps for Scotland (1910)

George Aitken – 2 caps for New Zealand (1921) and 8 caps for Scotland (1924-29)

Johnnie Wallace – 9 caps for Scotland (1923-26) and 8 caps for Australia (1921-28)

Doug Keller – 6 caps for Australia (1947-48) and 7 caps for Scotland (1949-50)

John Allan – 9 caps for Scotland (1990-91) and 13 caps for South Africa (1993-96)

91

The oldest rugby cup in the world

Edinburgh and Glasgow first contested an inter-city derby on 23 November 1872. The match was originally staged as an international trial and was won by Edinburgh by a goal to nil. In time, the inter-city competition was expanded to become an inter-district cup with the inclusion of the Borders and Caledonia.

The advent of professionalism ultimately saw an end to senior district teams as they once were – a change that was pronounced still further when both Caledonia and the Borders were disbanded as professional entities – and for many years the inter-city derby, although still part of the fixture list, didn't hold the same prestige as it once did. The SRU marketing department, however, was given a perfect hook around which to reignite the rivalry (and advertise and sell the home and away fixtures) when, in 2007, Glasgow back-row Stevie Swindall, who was helping in an office move in lieu of paying a fine for being late to a gym session, stumbled upon the 1872 Cup sitting at the back of a cupboard. The cup, officially the oldest in world rugby, is now a central part of the Pro14 calendar for both teams.

As a sidenote, back in 2007, as a reward for finding the cup and getting this whole train back on the tracks, Swindall was made to spend the afternoon cleaning it.

The trophy cabinet

While striving for Six Nations, Triple Crowns and World Cup titles (ahem), Scotland also exclusively contest the following trophies with other countries:

Calcutta Cup v England – first contested in 1879. The creation of the cup has already been discussed in item 15 of this book; it is a trophy famed throughout the rugby world, but perhaps the most infamous story about the cup occurred after the 1988 encounter in Edinburgh. After a fairly dire match that England won 9–6, the players got together for a post-match dinner that swiftly spiralled into a night out of epic proportions. 'All the tables had a load of booze on them that was virtually all gone by the time they even said grace,' recalled John Jeffrey. 'Four of our players were in bed before the end of the dinner. In retrospect, I wish I'd been one of them.

'After the dinner the captain used to take the Calcutta Cup out with them and you'd fill it with drinks all night and offer it around to punters to drink from. You'd get some pretty nasty mixes of drinks in there so it's not surprising that my memory of the whole night is fairly hazy. But I do remember bits and pieces. Dean Richards and I decided to fill the cup with whisky and then poured it over Brian Moore's head. He

The 'Calcutta Plate' the morning after.

started chasing us and we ran out of the pub and into a taxi, still with the cup. We went to another two or three pubs and then came back. I don't remember an awful lot after that.'

The cup started to be thrown around among fans and the players, with some witnesses alleging that it was drop-kicked down Rose Street – although Jeffrey and Richards deny this.

'All I can remember about it is that I was incredibly drunk,' said Richards. 'And that John Jeffrey and I took the Calcutta Cup out and it came back in a pretty bad state.'

'We headed back to our hotel eventually and I handed it in at reception,' said Jeffrey. 'When I woke up the next day all I could remember was the thing lying there behind the reception, battered to pieces.'

The incident of the 'Calcutta Plate', as it was renamed in the newspapers, raised considerable ire in the corridors of power at the RFU and the SRU, although their respective approaches to punishment were quite different. The RFU issued Richards with a one-week ban; the SRU, meanwhile, banned Jeffrey for five months.

'It's a chapter of my life that I am not terribly proud about,' said Jeffrey. 'But I'm still annoyed about how long my ban was compared to his.'

Centenary Quaich v Ireland – first contested in 1989, it marked a century of Test rugby matches between the two countries.

Hopetoun Cup v Australia – first contested in 1998. Named after the seventh Earl of Hopetoun, a Scotsman, who was the Governor General in Australia who presided over the Federation of Australia in 1901.

The Auld Alliance Trophy v France – first contested in 2018, it honours the internationals from both nations who died during the First World War. Twenty-one French players and thirty-one Scots died in the conflict, including Eric Milroy, who captained Scotland when the sides met in their last pre-war match, in Paris in 1913.

Doddie Weir Cup v Wales – introduced in the autumn of 2018, this is the first trophy to be exclusively contested between the old rivals in what will be only the second meeting between the countries outside the Five or Six Nations in the 135-year history of the fixture (the first was a World Cup warm-up in Cardiff in 2003 that Wales won 23–9).

Douglas Horn Trophy v Canada – first contested in 2008. Created to mark the long-standing relationship between Canada and Scotland and named after Douglas Horn, the father of Alan Horn who was a board member of Rugby Canada.

The ICBC Trophy v Argentina. This replaced its previous incarnation, the ICBC Cup, in 2016 and celebrates the friendship and history between the nations, who first played one another in 1969.

93

Longest winning streak

Scotland have only twice managed to put together a run of six consecutive wins (their best continuous winning sequence), which they achieved between 24 January 1925 and 6 February 1926 (beating, in the following order, France, Wales, Ireland, England, France and Wales before losing to Ireland on 27 February 1926), and between 28 October 1989 and 17 March 1990 (beating, in the following order, Fiji, Romania, Ireland, France, Wales and England before losing to New Zealand on 16 June 1990).

94

STAT ZONE

Longest losing streak

The 1951 Five Nations saw Scotland record one of the great victories of the era when they overcame the reigning Grand Slam champions Wales at Murrayfield 19–0, with prop Hamish Dawson scoring one try, wing Bob Gordon (making his debut) scoring two, number eight Peter Kininmonth landing an astonishing drop-goal and the other points coming from the boot of full-back Ian Thomson and lock Hamish Inglis. Between that glorious February day and the corresponding fixture in 1955, however, Scotland went on their longest run of consecutive defeats – 17 in total. During this dark period, they scored just 11 tries, six conversions, and four penalties for a paltry total of 57 points in five years, and endured humiliation at the hands of the Springboks in November 1951 in the 'Murrayfield Massacre', going down 44–0. It makes the Matt Williams era look positively rosy by comparison.

Welcome to the Hall of Fame

We have already talked about several Scottish members of the World Rugby Hall of Fame in some depth (Jim Greenwood, Bill Maclagan, David Bedell-Sivright, Gavin Hastings, Ned Haig and Melrose RFC) but there are several other notable inclusions in this exalted group. They are: Ian McGeechan (40 caps, 1972-79, inducted 2009), Andy Irvine (60 caps, 1972-84, inducted 2015), Gordon Brown (38 caps, 1969-77, inducted 2015), GPS Macpherson (26 caps, 1922-32, inducted 2016), and the legendary commentator Bill McLaren (inducted 2015).

Award winners and nominees

Stuart Hogg won Player of the Six Nations in 2016 and 2017 after some mind-blowing performances. Since the creation of the award in 2004, Hogg is the only Scottish winner.

Mike Blair, meanwhile, became the first Scot to be nominated for IRB World Player of the Year, in 2008, but he was beaten to the title by Shane Williams. Greig Laidlaw became the second and, so far, last Scot nominated for the award when he was listed in 2015, but he too lost out in the final reckoning as the award went to Dan Carter.

STAT ZONE

The luck of (playing) the Irish

While Irish rugby is currently enjoying a long run of success that began at the turn of the century (and has included a number of thumping wins over Scotland), in the early years of Test rugby, Scotland dominated the annual fixture against Ireland, losing just once in 16 years. The results began to be shared more equally thereafter, with Scotland enjoying a marginally better win ratio until 1926 (winning 16 to Ireland's nine between 1894 and 1925), before Ireland began to dominate the fixture more regularly – including a run of nine consecutive wins from 1939 to 1954. This trend was then reversed in the 1990s when for ten years – between 1989 and 1999 – Scotland didn't lose once to the men in green, notching up 11 victories and drawing once. Since the millennium, however, things have swung back the other way, with Scotland defeating Ireland just six times in 18 years.

Notable losses

A tough but familiar subject this one – discussing some of Scotland's heaviest and most notable defeats over the years. Unfortunately, there are many to choose from, but here is a selection of some of the worst:

1951: The Murrayfield Massacre. The touring Springboks visited Murrayfield and tore Scotland apart, winning 44–0 and scoring nine tries, seven conversions and a drop-goal. It was said of this game that Scotland were lucky to have scored nil.

1997: The Springboks were back to inflict even more pain on Scotland in 1997 as they looked to reclaim their crown as the world's best team after it had slipped with consecutive series defeats at home to the All Blacks in 1996 and to the Lions in the summer of '97. If they wanted to make a statement, they certainly did that day, winning 68-10 and scoring ten tries through Rassie Erasmus, Percy Montgomery (two), Pieter Rossouw, James Small (two), Franco Smith, Andre Snyman, Gary Teichmann and Andre Venter, plus eight conversions by Montgomery and one from Jannie de Beer.

Some other 'highlights' of Springbok shellackings are:
1994: 34–10 at Murrayfield

1998: 35–10 at Murrayfield

1999: 46–29 at Murrayfield

2004: 45–10 at Murrayfield

2006: 36–16 at Kings Park

2006: 29–15 at Port Elizabeth

2007: 27–3 at Murrayfield

2013: 28–0 at Murrayfield

2014: 55–6 at Nelson Mandela Bay Stadium

2015: 34–16 at St James' Park

The Springboks are not alone in giving Scotland a good southern hemisphere thrashing, as Australia and, especially, New Zealand have proved over the years. Below are some of the worst hidings we've suffered at their hands:

V Australia

1970: 23–3 at the Sydney Cricket Ground

1982: 33–9 at the Sydney Cricket Ground

1984: 37–12 at Murrayfield

1988: 32–13 at Murrayfield

1992: 27–12 at the Sydney Cricket Ground

1992: 37–13 at Ballymore

1997: 37–8 at Murrayfield

1998: 45–3 at the Sydney Football Stadium

1998: 33–11 at Suncorp Stadium

2000: 30–9 at Murrayfield

2003: 33–16 at Suncorp Stadium

2004: 35–15 at the Etihad Stadium

2004: 34–13 at Stadium Australia

2004: 31–14 at Murrayfield

2004: 31–17 at Hampden Park

2006: 44–15 at Murrayfield

V New Zealand

1981: 40–15 at Eden Park

1987: 30–3 at Lancaster Park

1990: 31–16 at Carisbrook

1993: 51–15 at Murrayfield

1996: 62–31 at Carisbrook

1996: 36–12 at Eden Park

2000: 69–20 at Carisbrook

2000: 48–14 at Eden Park

2001: 37–6 at Murrayfield

2007: 40–0 at Murrayfield

2008: 32–6 at Murrayfield

2010: 49–3 at Murrayfield

2012: 51–22 at Murrayfield

Each of our traditional Five Nations rivals have also inflicted a number of sobering defeats on Scotland over the years.

In 2000, Italy were welcomed into the expanded Six Nations and celebrated by defeating the 1999 Five Nations champions 34–20 in Rome. Scotland have lost several times to Italy over the years, although the most memorable of these is surely the Six Nations loss at Murrayfield in 2007 when Scotland gifted two intercept tries and a charge-down in a chaotic first half, which gave Italy a 21–0 lead, which they used as a springboard to a 37–17 final score.

England are, of course, Scotland's oldest (and bitterest) rivals and over the course of nearly 150 years of playing each other, they have recorded some chastening scorelines over their northern foes. Throughout the amateur era, the tussles between the sides were mostly closely fought affairs, but after the game went pro in 1995, England began to record some devastating scores in the fixture.

V England
1924: 19–0 at Twickenham
1947: 24–5 at Twickenham
1949: 19–3 at Twickenham
1977: 26–6 at Twickenham
1992: 25–7 at Murrayfield
1993: 26–12 at Twickenham
1997: 41–13 at Twickenham
1998: 34–20 at Murrayfield
2001: 43–3 at Twickenham
2002: 29–3 at Murrayfield
2003: 40–9 at Twickenham
2004: 35–13 at Murrayfield
2005: 43–22 at Twickenham
2007: 42–20 at Twickenham
2013: 38–18 at Twickenham
2014: 20–0 at Murrayfield
2017: 61–21 at Twickenham

In recent years, Wales have dished out some real humiliations to Scotland in Cardiff, in particular in 2014 and 2018 – but unfortunately, these thumping triumphs do not stand in isolation.

V Wales
1904: 21–3 at St Helen's, Swansea
1911: 32–19 at Inverleith

1912: 21–6 at St Helen's, Swansea

1914: 24–5 at the Arms Park

1972: 35–12 at the Arms Park

1976: 28–6 at the Arms Park

1994: 29–6 at the Arms Park

2005: 46–22 at Murrayfield

2014: 51–3 at the Millennium Stadium

2018: 34–7 at the Principality Stadium

Similarly, Ireland have enjoyed some thumping wins over Scotland since the turn of the century, having long been the underdog in the fixture.

V Ireland

1950: 21–0 at Lansdowne Road

1953: 26–8 at Murrayfield

2000: 44–22 at Lansdowne Road

2002: 43–22 at Lansdowne Road

2003: 36–6 at Murrayfield

2003: 29–10 at Murrayfield

2004: 37–16 at Lansdowne Road

2005: 40–13 at Murrayfield

2008: 34–13 at Croke Park

2012: 32–14 at Aviva Stadium

2014: 28–6 at Aviva Stadium

2015: 40–10 at Murrayfield

2018: 28–8 at Aviva Stadium

Our Auld Alliance brethren across the Channel have also got in on the act. Scotland made history when we became the first of the Home Union sides to lose to France, in 1911, and although it took several decades before France became a true powerhouse Test nation, once they had established themselves as such, they have given Scotland some real pastings down the years.

V France
1977: 23–3 at the Parc des Princes
1997: 47–20 at the Parc des Princes
1998: 51–16 at Murrayfield
2003: 38–3 at the Stade de France
2003: 51–9 at Stadium Australia
2004: 31–0 at Murrayfield
2007: 46–19 at the Stade de France
2008: 27–6 at Murrayfield

There have also been some other notable losses to teams outside the traditional rugby powers. In 1998, Scotland lost 51–16 to Fiji in Suva, and lost there again in 2018, going down 27–22.

Along with the losses to Fiji, there have also been prominent losses to several of the other so-called 'minnows' of world rugby:

V Romania
1984: 28–22 at the Dinamo Stadium, Bucharest
1991: 18–12 at the Dinamo Stadium, Bucharest

V Japan
1989: 28–24 at the Chichibunomiya Rugby Stadium, Tokyo

John Barclay holds his head after losing to Argentina at the 2011 World Cup.

V Samoa

1993: 21–10 in Apia

2013: 27–17 at King's Park, Durban

V Argentina

1969: 20–3 at Gimnasia y Esgrima, Buenos Aires

1999: 31–22 at Murrayfield

2007: 19–13 at the Stade de France (World Cup quarter-final)

2011: 13–12 Wellington Regional Stadium, Wellington (World Cup pool match)

V Canada

1991: 24–19 at Saint John, New Brunswick

2002: 26–23 at the Thunderbird Stadium, Vancouver

V Tonga

2012: 21–15 at Pittodrie, Aberdeen

V USA

2018: 30–29 at the BBVA Compass Stadium, Houston

99

Biggest wins away from home

While securing wins away from home are a little thin on the ground for the current Scotland team, there have been some notable triumphs on the road throughout history. Here are some of the highlights:

Twickenham, 1983. Scotland 22, England 12

Cardiff, 1982. Scotland 34, Wales 18

Dublin, 1984. Scotland 32, Ireland 9

Paris, 1999. Scotland 36, France 22

Sydney, 2017. Scotland 24, Australia 19

Resistencia, 2018. Scotland 44, Argentina 15

100

FAMOUS FIRSTS

An artificial game

Scotland's 2014 win against Tonga at Rugby Park in Kilmarnock was the first international to be played on an artificial surface. Scotland won 37–12 with tries from Blair Cowan, Stuart Hogg, Alex Dunbar, Geoff Cross and Tommy Seymour, with Greig Laidlaw converting three of these and slotting two penalties.

Alex Dunbar on the charge against Tonga at Rugby Park.

It's in the blood

Scottish rugby is littered with familial ties as players have followed their fathers, brothers and grandfathers into the blue jersey.

Fathers and sons
John (25 caps, 1980-87) and Johnnie (38 caps, 2006-15) **Beattie**
John (2 caps, 1913-1920) and Rab (3 caps, 1937-39) and Logie (5 caps, 1948-53) **Bruce-Lockhart**
Mike (31 caps, 1961-66) and Jeremy (3 caps, 1986-87) **Campbell-Lamerton**
Alastair (2 caps, 1947) and Colin (5 caps, 1975-76) **Fisher**
Robert (8 caps 1920-21) and George (1 cap 1939) **Gallie**
Irvine (6 caps, 1906-08) and Keith (4 caps, 1947) **Geddes**
Henry (6 caps, 1894-99) and Peter (1 cap, 1933) **Gedge**
Ron (10 caps, 1962-65) and Cameron (1 cap, 1997) **Glasgow**
Gavin (67 caps, 1986-1995) and Adam (3 caps, 2018) **Hastings**
Jack (6 caps, 1951-55) and Brian (4 caps, 1978) **Hegarty**
Sandy (21 caps, 1966-70) and Ben (18 caps, 2002-05) **Hinshelwood**
Alan (15 caps, 1972-80) and Rory (31 caps, 2006-2012) **Lawson**
Max (28 caps, 1926-32) and Brian (7 caps, 1965-71) **Simmers**
Allen (9 caps, 1914-21) and Donald (7 caps, 1950-53) **Sloan**
Herbert (18 caps, 1924-30) and Gordon (20 caps, 1957-62) **Waddell**
Joseph (2 caps, 1904) and Frank (7 caps, 1930-32) **Waters**

Brothers
Robert (7 caps, 1879-82) and Thomas (1881-85) **Ainslie**
John (2 caps, 1871-72) and Allen (2 caps, 1875-76) **Arthur**
David (23 caps, 1900-08) and John (1 cap, 1902) **Bedell-Sivright**

Cameron (3 caps, 1963) and Alasdair (6 caps, 1966-68) **Boyle**

Peter (27 caps, 1964-73) and Gordon (38 caps, 1969-77) **Brown**

Logie (5 caps, 1948-53) and Rab (3 caps, 1937-39) **Bruce Lockhart**

Gordon (77 caps, 1997-2005) and Alan (5 caps, 2000-01) **Bulloch**

Jim (28 caps, 1981-85) and Finlay (37 caps, 1986-91) **Calder**

Angus (19 caps, 1948-56) and Donald (6 caps, 1953-54) **Cameron**

David (14 caps, 1964-68) and Robin (11 caps, 1955-60) **Chisholm**

George (1 cap, 1904) and Jack (6 caps, 1900-05) **Crabbie**

William (2 caps, 1871-72) and Malcolm (9 caps, 1875-80) **Cross**

Jimmy (1 cap, 1910) and John (6 caps, 1911-12) **Dobson**

John (8 caps, 1895-97) and Francis (1 cap, 1901) **Dods**

Peter (23 caps, 1983-91) and Michael (8 caps, 1994-96) **Dods**

Andrew (13 caps, 1881-88) and Patrick (6 caps, 1885-87) **Don Wauchope**

Arthur (15 caps, 1950-57) and Tom (5 caps, 1938-39) **Dorward**

Jimmy (20 caps, 1922-29) and Andrew (1 cap, 1932) **Dykes**

Christy (12 caps, 1958-65) and Tom (5 caps, 1968-70) **Elliot**

Thom (10 caps, 2008-10) and Max (44 caps, 2008-14) **Evans**

Zander (18 caps, 2016-18) and Matt (1 cap, 2018) **Fagerson**

James (4 caps, 1871-75), Arthur (1 cap, 1875) and Ninian (9 caps, 1875-1881) **Finlay**

Bryan (3 caps 1980-83) and Jim (1 cap 1980) **Gossman**

Oliver (6 caps, 1960-64) and Derrick (14 caps, 1965-68) **Grant**

Richie (66 caps, 2010-18) and Jonny (43 caps, 2013-18) **Gray**

Gavin (67 caps, 1986-95) and Scott (67 caps, 1986-97) **Hastings**

Ian (8 caps, 1939-48) and Mac (3 caps, 1933) **Henderson**

Peter (35 caps, 2013-18) and George (2 caps, 2018) **Horne**

Bob (11 caps, 1924-25) and Dave (7 caps, 1912-13) **Howie**

Robert (13 caps, 1871-80) and Duncan (3 caps, 1878-79) **Irvine**

Sean (105 caps, 2004-16) and Rory (29 caps, 2005-12) **Lamont**

John (23 caps, 1998-2002) and Martin (37 caps, 1998-2003) **Leslie**

James (1 cap, 1872) and George (1 cap, 1873) **McClure**

Bill (18 caps, 1894-1903) and Saxon (15 caps, 1886-92) **McEwan**

Duncan (3 caps, 1907) and Ian (1 cap, 1909) **MacGregor**

Lewis (6 caps, 1904-05) and Ken (10 caps, 1905-08) **MacLeod**

Robert (5 caps, 1881-85) and Gardyne (2 caps, 1885) **Maitland**

Tom (4 caps, 1871-74) and William (1 cap, 1872) **Marshall**

Iain (44 caps, 1979-90), Kenny (40 caps, 1989-95) and David (1 cap, 1991) **Milne**

George (2 caps, 1921-26) and Ronald (2 caps, 1935) **Murray**
William (14 caps, 1891-97), George (14 caps, 1891-96), Gordon (1 cap, 1894) and Robert (6 caps, 1898-1900) **Neilson**
Charles (16 caps, 1887-82) and John (12 caps, 1889-93) **Orr**
Alex (10 caps, 1906-08) and William (6 caps, 1912-13) **Purves**
Charles (21 caps, 1881-88) and James (5 caps, 1874-77) **Reid**
James (1901-03, 5 caps) and Edward (1 cap, 1904) **Ross**
Wilson (19 caps, 1934-39) and Ian (1 cap, 1937) **Shaw**
Alexander (1 cap, 1911) and William (1 cap, 1925) **Stevenson**
Charles (7 caps, 1909-11) and Ludovic (8 caps, 1923-30) **Stuart**
Dave (2 caps, 1947) and Alec (3 caps, 1953) **Valentine**
Archibald (5 caps, 1881-83) and James (2 caps, 1882-3) **Walker**
Jack (1 cap, 1914) and Ronald (5 caps, 1922-30) **Warren**

Brother and sister
Craig (61 caps, 1989-1999) and Paula (75 caps, 1994-2006) **Chalmers**

Grandfathers and grandsons
John **Bannerman** (37 caps, 1921-29) and Shade **Munro** (7 caps, 1994-97)
George **Ritchie** (1 cap, 1932) and Andy **Nicol** (23 caps, 1992-2001)

ALSO AVAILABLE FROM

★POLARIS
PUBLISHING

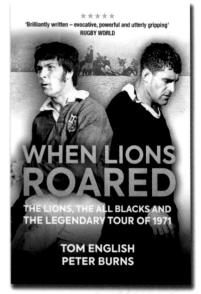

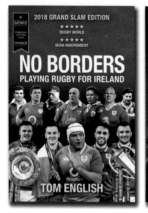

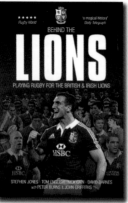